# MEMORY
# BOOSTER
# WORKOUT

# MEMORY BOOSTER WORKOUT

## 10 STEPS TO A POWERFUL MEMORY

Dr. Jo Iddon

Dr. Huw Williams

THUNDER BAY
P·R·E·S·S

San Diego, California

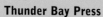

**Thunder Bay Press**
An imprint of the Advantage Publishers Group
5880 Oberlin Drive, San Diego, CA 92121-4794
www.thunderbaybooks.com

All notations of errors or omissions should be addressed
to Thunder Bay Press, Editorial Department, at the above
address. All other correspondence (author inquiries,
permissions) concerning the content of this book should
be addressed to Hamlyn, a division of Octopus Publishing
Group Ltd., 2–4 Heron Quays, London E14 4JP, U.K.

ISBN 1-57145-989-8

Library of Congress Cataloging-in-Publication Data available
upon request.

Printed in Italy
1  2  3  4  5  07  06  05  04  03

# CONTENTS

# INTRODUCTION

How often do you forget someone's name or what you went into a room for? Or perhaps you find you get that "tip-of-the-tongue" feeling just a little too often when you are trying to recall a name. You may feel that sometimes your memory surprises you with its speed and clarity, but at other times it lets you down. Perhaps you feel that you have a poor memory, or you may be getting older and becoming concerned that your memory is failing you. Well, memory is a puzzle to us all, but one of the best ways to try to improve it is to understand more about its nature.

## SO WHAT IS MEMORY?

Memory is the process by which our brains store information about the world in order to give us a sense of who we are. What is stored in our memories is specific and personal because we are all unique.

## HOW DOES MEMORY WORK?

Scientists have studied the processes of memory in detail using different techniques. They have learned that memory can be broken down into three main stages: **encoding**—taking information in, **storage**—storing information, and **retrieval**—finding information from our stores when we need it.

We have different types of memory stores for different occasions, including **short-term active memory,** which filters out irrelevant information and keeps things in mind just long enough, for example, to dial a telephone number. **Long-term memory** is a highly durable and organized memory store. Within this store there are substores for specific "episodes" in our lives and for more general factual information.

Our memories are highly organized and we can often improve our recall by adding meaning and structure to information that we take in. Memory does not work in isolation, and factors such as **concentration, planning,** and **organization** play a crucial role in memory function.

Memory can also be vulnerable and is affected by a multitude of factors, for example, how old you are, what sex you are, and how happy you are. In fact, anything that affects our brains affects our memories. What we eat, how much alcohol we drink, how often we fly, and being pregnant can all affect our memories in different ways.

## HOW TO USE THIS BOOK

This book is designed to help you improve your memory in ten steps. To get the most out of the book you should start with step one and work systematically through to step ten, making sure you have understood each step before you move on to the next. The first half of the book describes what memory is and what factors affect it—these are important concepts to understand and are the first steps to improving your memory. You will then be guided to study your own memory in detail through exercises and memory tasks. The second half of the book focuses on different ways of improving your memory, including the development of strategies and advice on how to use them in specific situations.

## WHAT YOU CAN EXPECT TO ACHIEVE FROM READING THIS BOOK

- An understanding of the underlying processes of memory and how vulnerable our memories are to different factors
- An understanding of your own personal memory profile—specific strengths and weaknesses
- Different types of strategies to improve your memory in different situations
- An understanding of how different lifestyle factors can affect your memory and how to improve in these areas

The quick reference guide in step ten will act as a useful summary and refresher for the future. But remember, improving your memory is a bit like improving your physical health—it takes time, discipline, and effort. Good luck!

# UNDERSTANDING MEMORY

*Memory is a storage place* in our brains. It is personal and gives us history. It tells us what we did yesterday, as well as ten years ago, and it knows what we are doing tomorrow. Memories of childhood may be triggered from hearing a nursery rhyme, or a romantic memory may come to mind when we smell a particular kind of flower. Memory uses all kinds of clues to give us a sense of who we are.

*The study of memory has a long history. Today our most sophisticated technologies are being used to study it. As we answer some questions, others naturally follow. In this book we aim to tell you what is known about memory and how you may help its capabilities. We will start with how we have come to know about memory and what the word "memory" has come to mean.*

# How do we know about memory?

## USING PSYCHOLOGICAL TESTS

Scientists, particularly neuropsychologists, have developed many approaches to the study of memory. One method for studying memory is to give people tests to see how they respond and what may interfere with their performance. For example, they might show people some pictures and then see if they can distinguish them from other pictures they have not seen. This is called **visual recognition memory**. Or, they might read out a list of words and ask people to repeat them. This is called **verbal recall**.

Using these types of tests, it has been found that, on average, people can recall approximately seven words (or other types of information such as numbers), and they find it easier to recall the first and last few items. If the information is organized in some way, such as by category, then people can often recall much more and for a longer period of time. By using these sorts of tests, psychologists have put together models of how they think the memory system works.

# BRAIN AND MEMORY DISORDERS

Much of our knowledge about memory has been learned from studying people with brain disorders. This has also helped clinicians develop better techniques for diagnosis and rehabilitation in brain disorders.

Amnesiacs have also been a great help to science. Amnesia is when a part (or parts) of the brain that has a function in supporting a part of the memory system becomes damaged. Such individuals are often able to describe how they are experiencing the world in a different way from how they used to. Their brain function can also be assessed using objective tests that measure different types of memory.

So, from these types of cases, as well as other memory disorders, scientists have built up profiles of different types of memory processing and of the brain areas that are important to memory.

 ## Brain imaging (neuroradiology)

Brain imaging is a development that has proved useful in the study of memory. It gives us a real image of where memory is located in the brain.

• Basic scanning methods such as **computed tomography (CAT or CT) scans** show structures in the brain by sending X rays across the brain tissue. Combining pictures of damaged brains with results from memory tests has helped us learn more about where memory happens.

• **Functional Magnetic Resonance Imaging (fMRI)** can be used to track ongoing changes in the brain as the person is asked to do something, such as remember a list of words. FMRI does this by picking up magnetic "markers" of brain activity, such as taking up oxygen. It has given us the technology to actually "see" memory working in real time.

• Another current type of "active" scan, called **Positron Emission Tomography (PET) scanning**, shows changes in blood flow and brain chemicals during memory tasks. This has helped scientists learn about how chemical systems within the brain interact with physical structures in memory research.

# HOW
# MEMORY WORKS

*This book focuses* on crucial ways of understanding memory for everyday life. There are three main processes of memory: **encoding** (getting memories in), **storage** (keeping memories), and **retrieval** (getting memories out again). Memory is an activity that is dynamic and ever-present, and we are only just beginning to formulate theories and ideas about how to put the memory jigsaw puzzle together. This growing body of knowledge is already helping us to improve our capacity to remember.

### MEMORY IS ACTIVE

While it may be doing one thing that you are aware of, memory is also doing lots of other things. It works at many levels.

### The brain and memory

The processes of memory, of course, take place in the brain. Different kinds of information are received and stored in different locations.

- Working, or short-term, memory processing probably happens in the front part of the brain.
- The process of storing new memories (that is, learning) takes place in the temporal lobes on the sides of the brain.
- The big outer part of the brain (called the cortex) is probably where memories are stored.
- Visual information comes in through our eyes and is processed by the back part of the brain, called the occipital lobe.
- Auditory information comes in through the ears and is processed by the temporal lobes.
- Spatial information is processed by the parietal lobe, at the top of the brain.
- There are also special areas that are involved in emotional memory processing, language, and habits.
- The left side of the brain is involved more in verbal memory, and the right side more in visual memory.

# Donkeys don't hop.

## MEMORY IS COMPLEX

Memory is made up of many components that work together to bring a sense of the past into mind to deal with the present and plan for the future.

## EXPLICIT AND IMPLICIT MEMORIES

As children, we learn that there are things that have four legs and a tail and are called cats. A child sees a donkey and says "cat." The child is told, "No, it has big ears and eats carrots and so is a donkey." The parent reinforces correct responses and corrects wrong responses. The child sees a rabbit, which eats carrots. The child says "donkey" and is corrected to say "rabbit, it hops," and so on. So there are descriptions attached to the concepts as they group up: Small carrot-eaters that hop are rabbits, big carrot-eaters that bray are donkeys, and small, four-legged creatures with tails are cats.

Although language starts off in this way as being explicitly learned, that is, word by word, it soon becomes an implicit vocabulary that follows complex rules that we can't describe. Much of our knowledge starts off as explicit learning by awareness—how to speak, how to ride a bicycle, and so on. Over time, this learning becomes implicit, and we would find it very difficult to describe exactly how we learned certain skills or habits. This is because once a memory becomes implicit, it becomes automatic.

 ## Tricks of memory

People are often puzzled by the tricks played on them by their memory, such as forgetting vital things at crucial moments and remembering unwanted things at awkward times. You may be rushing to an important lunch date, and stop to get money out of an ATM. For some reason, you just can't quite remember your personal identification number. You try three times and your card is retained. How are you going to explain this to the bank? "What is wrong with me?" will go through your head, and you feel even more stressed. Typically, you will remember the personal identification number a few minutes later. The truth is that we all do this type of thing from time to time, and it is more than likely just the stress of the moment suppressing your recall.

# SHORT-TERM
## MEMORY

*The simplest way* to understand short-term memory is to consider it as information that is in our consciousness; it is the memory garnered from things and events we have recently experienced. ***Short-term memory*** is the tool we use to remember phone numbers for just long enough to dial them, or directions to an unfamiliar destination.

## THE MEMORY FILTER

We take information in through our senses into our brain. Our consciousness only allows in what is needed—the rest is filtered out. Right now you might be sitting in your living room, only aware of the words you are reading. Stop for a moment, and make yourself aware of what is actually going on around you—perhaps your partner turning the pages of a newspaper, the smell of sausages cooking, the sound of a child playing next door, or the constant hum of your computer in the background.

Return your focus to reading and gradually the noises become irrelevant again and don't distract you. Your short-term memory is back to concentrating on your reading. This filter is a crucial part of the memory system, as it keeps our minds from becoming overloaded with irrelevant information.

## CAPACITY OF SHORT-TERM MEMORY

Short-term memory has only a limited capacity, with about seven spaces, or "slots." For example, you could probably remember the names of about seven people, but once there were more names, you would start to forget. To keep something in your short-term memory, you need to work at it (it is sometimes also called **working memory**). For example, if you look up a phone number, you will need to repeat it to yourself in order to remember it long enough to dial it. This technique is known as **rehearsal**. After just a few moments, the phone number will be replaced in your consciousness by new information coming in.

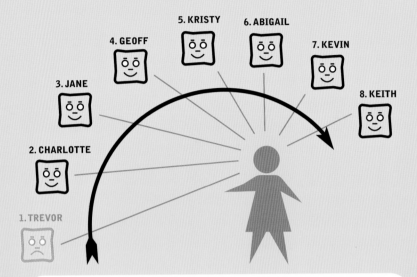

Sarah is introduced to a group of eight people: Trevor, Charlotte, Jane, Geoff, Kristy, Abigail, Kevin, and Keith. As she hears each name, Sarah registers it in an available slot in her short-term memory, which previously was empty. Once Kevin is introduced, all seven of Sarah's short-term memory slots are full. When the eighth person, Keith, is introduced and processed, Trevor is forgotten or displaced.

# ENCODING INFORMATION

Information is encoded into our short-term memory in several ways.

**VISUAL CODE** We try to picture the person's name or imagine him or her wearing a hat. The image starts to fade away after a few moments unless we keep the image active.

**ACOUSTIC CODE** This is the most common technique used to keep information active in our short-term memory. It involves repeating the information, such as a name or a number.

**SEMANTIC CODE** This is where we use a meaningful association, for example thinking of a familiar person who shares the same name.

# CONCENTRATION

Short-term memory is transient and easily interrupted. Therefore, concentration is an important ingredient for keeping things in mind. It may only be when you get distracted that you become aware that you are "actively" remembering. Here are two common examples:

### Phone numbers

You look up a phone number from your address book. Just as you are about to dial the number, you hear someone come in through the front door. It is likely that you will have to look up the number again. This is because your active memory has been interrupted and you have momentarily lost concentration.

### What did I come in here for?

You are in the kitchen organizing some papers and you decide you need a stapler. As you walk to the study to get the stapler, you start to think about what you might cook for supper that evening. When you arrive at the study, you can't remember what you have gone in there for. Again, you have simply become distracted.

# SUBLIMINAL MEMORY

Information can pass through the filter without us knowing that it has gone in. For example, in the 1960s, television advertising executives came up with the clever concept of subliminal advertising. A picture of a product, for example, a particular brand of laundry detergent, would be "flashed" on the television screen for a very brief moment. It could be at any time, even in the middle of a film. It would be so quick that we would not consciously be aware of what we had seen, but subliminally our memory would have stored the picture.

Next time you were in the supermarket, that brand of laundry detergent would seem familiar. This would distinguish it from the other products, encouraging a sale. Concerns grew that such techniques could be used (or perhaps actually even were being used) to brainwash people, and the technique was made illegal.

# LONG-TERM
## MEMORY

*If a short-term memory* is important enough to endure, it is stored in the long-term memory. To get an idea of how the long-term memory works, imagine a memory going through a front door, into a hallway (short-term memory), and then into a room where it is sorted and stored. This "memory store" is huge, with many interconnecting rooms and an almost infinite capacity.

## MEMORY RETRIEVAL

The memory store is organized, but not as neatly as a library. When we want to retrieve information, we need to search for it. Sometimes we find what we are looking for right away; at other times it takes longer.

Occasionally, you may not be able to find what you are looking for at all. This is partly because the more you learn, the more competition there is when you are trying to retrieve information. Imagine a bag of marbles. When there are only a few marbles, each one is distinct and easy to identify. The more marbles that are added, the harder it is to distinguish between them.

## RETRIEVAL FAILURE

Sometimes we fail to retrieve information that we know we have.

**Tip-of-the-tongue phenomenon**—you are sure you know the answer to a question, but you can't quite get ahold of it.

**Encoding error**—sometimes we don't encode well enough the information we want to retrieve later. You think you have understood something, but when you try to explain it to someone else, you find that you have not understood it as well as you thought and there are gaps.

# *All the witnesses to a car accident will remember something different.*

## REMEMBERING THE FUTURE

You also need to be aware of a rather odd kind of memory in which your long-term memory and short-term memory combine forces. This is your memory for the future (regarding things that have not yet happened), known as **prospective memory**. This involves being aware of what you are doing next week or next month, as well as your plans, hopes, and dreams for the future.

### Eyewitness testimony

We tend to "dynamically re-create" some memory stories, filling in the gaps and warping our memories to fit particular situations. Different types of information cue recall from different types of memory stores. This has been shown in eyewitness testimony research.

The car "went" by.

The car "sped" by.

- **Undue influence**—if asked "How fast was the car going when it sped past you?" rather than "What was the speed of the car as it went by?" a witness will tend to give a faster estimated speed. We are notoriously bad at judging speed, but a leading word such as "sped" rather than "went" triggers a memory association of greater speed.

- **Memory distortion**—if a policeman asks you to describe the scene of a car accident after the cars "crashed" into each other, rather than simply "collided" or "bumped," you are much more likely to report that you saw blood, even if no one was injured.

# MEMORY STORES

*Our brains have evolved* to have separate parts to deal with information that comes from different senses or different time periods, and that have different levels of importance. A friend's birthday, the way to a business appointment, and a shopping list will all be stored in a different part of the memory.

### The passage of time

As time passes, your conscious experience stays focused on the here and now. Whatever was just in your conscious experience passes on into another part of your memory system, or is discarded. Your current, short-term memory is focused on reading. But you can remember that you went to see a movie last night, and this is your memory for a particular life episode (remembering the events of one's life is called **autobiographical memory**). You can remember the key actor in the film. In a month's time, you will remember that you saw the film, but probably only the gist of the story. In a year's time, you might rent a film on video and after it begins, remember that you have already seen it.

| NOW | AFTER SIX MONTHS | AFTER ONE YEAR |
|---|---|---|
|  |  |  |
| "I saw *The Third Man* starring Orson Welles last night." | "I saw *The Third Man* starring, er, what's his name...?" | "I might have seen *The Third Man* once." |

## TYPES OF MEMORY STORE

There are two main types of storage for explicit memories.

- **Semantic**—this is the store for general world knowledge. It is a bit like an ever-growing encyclopedia within the brain. Any type of factual knowledge is semantic in nature, including facts (e.g., Paris is the capital of France) and also more basic knowledge about the world (e.g., a robin is a bird).

- **Episodic**—this is a more personal memory for episodes and events: what we did last night or for our eighteenth birthday party, where we went on our summer vacation, etc.

# OTHER TYPES
## OF MEMORY

*There are three* other templates within memory, and they help us to function successfully in our normal day-to-day lives. They are **memory scripts**, **memory schemas**, and **mental maps**.

## MEMORY SCHEMAS

Memory schemas are collections of actions that are **activated automatically** with the appropriate trigger. For example, if you are driving a car and you see a red traffic light ahead, you automatically start braking.

## MEMORY SCRIPTS

Memory scripts relate to the events that occur in a **particular social setting**. They influence appropriate behavior and are the sort of generalized memory needed in order to cope with everyday situations. For example, when you go to a restaurant, you know that you often wait to be seated, that you are shown a menu and order choices from it, that you have a waiter or waitress who takes your order, that things are served in a particular sequence, and that you get a bill at the end.

## MENTAL MAPS

Our **knowledge about our environment** is also organized into mental maps. For example, when you move to a new area it will seem strange and you will not know your way around. After you live there for a few weeks, however, you will gradually become more and more familiar with the layout of the streets, where you can go shopping, and how to get around. You effectively build up a mental map.

|  | Memory schema | Memory script | Mental map |
|---|---|---|---|
| **Event:** | Traffic lights ahead turn red | Go to a restaurant or cafe for lunch | Move to a new area |
| **Action:** | Automatically start braking | Know that food is ordered off the menu from a waiter or waitress | Gradually become familiar with the streets surrounding your home |

*You hear the doorbell, so you answer the door.*

*You wouldn't do the dishes after eating in a restaurant.*

*You can find your way to work without a map.*

# FORMS OF
# INFORMATION

*Information can be* verbal, visual, tactile, olfactory, or emotional. *Some parts of the brain are specialized for processing these different kinds of information, and other parts for associating them—with the end goal of integrating the information. For example, the chemical compound that wafts up your nose and into your olfactory center becomes the smell of a rose when it is recognized by your memory system. It then cascades into other associations, such as that time you picked roses from your aunt's garden.*

*One kind of cue can trigger all kinds of other memories. There has been some research to show that different cues can work to make memories more vivid, depending on how old people are. In research on autobiographical memory, for example, if a younger person is given a word or a smell to cue a memory, they rate the memories pretty much the same for vividness. However, if the different cues are given to an older person, the smell cue tends to trigger more vivid memories. If you want to have control over the connections, you need to be aware of these associations. Indeed, you can use them to help your powers of recall.*

### Test your autobiographical memory

Think of an episode from your past that is conjured up by any of the following words:

- River
- Hospital
- Garden
- Betrayal
- Paris

# REMEMBERING IS PERSONAL

Dreams, thought, actions, names, places, faces, smells, facts, feelings, tastes, and much more are brought into our consciousness through remembering. There are different modalities to our memories. Sometimes memories are more distinctly one type than another; at other times they are a kaleidoscope of flavors, textures, and sounds. In a way, memory is like a web woven from sounds, smells, tastes, touches, and sights.

When you are trying to recall information, memory will try to take shortcuts to help with the job of remembering by making associations. What emerges from much research, however, is that it is your personal knowledge, motivation, and the meaning of things to you that drives your memory. It is what helps give memory meaning.

### Sense of self

"To be or not to be, that is the question." Most people know that this quote is from Shakespeare's *Hamlet.* If you are familiar with the story, you will know that these words were spoken at a particularly charged moment. Yet these words will not be as important to you as when your children uttered their first words or when your partner first told you that he or she loved you. You may conjure up a scene more dramatic than Shakespeare's, because it was yours. That place, that perfume, that feeling you had—and, as you remember it, you may get a faraway look and a heartfelt surge of emotion.

Memory is the most personal thing we have. It gives us our sense of self. At the heart of memory, then, there is you. Memory works largely on the principle of "Is this now or will it at some point be personally relevant to me?" This "higher" type of memory is what we sometimes call **conscious feeling**.

# *You are what you remember.*

# UNDERSTANDING
## WHAT AFFECTS MEMORY

*Various factors affect the way* the memory functions, and to improve your memory's performance, you will need to appreciate which of these factors are most relevant to you, and why it is sometimes necessary for us to forget certain things. Forgetting is defined as the inability to recall, recognize, or reproduce that which was previously learned—in other words, drawing a complete blank when you are asked something like "What were you doing last Monday?"

## Forgetting

Forgetting is normal—we don't actually need to remember everything. Without forgetting, your head would be spinning, with far too much information in it. So forgetting is, in fact, crucial to remembering, since you need to free up your memory for the things you want or need to remember.

### WHY DO WE NEED TO FORGET THINGS?

There are three main reasons why we forget.

**1. Decayed memories**

Information in the sensory store tends to decay rapidly. If it has got through to the working memory—into the acoustic or the visual storage—it will stay there for perhaps thirty or forty seconds, but it will disappear unless it is actively worked on. In the acoustic store, this means repeating or rehearsing what was said or read. In the visual store, this means visual manipulation of the images. If information is not being actively worked on in the short-term memory, it just vanishes.

**2. Interference**

Items in short-term memory may become victims of interference from new information already coming in. Can you remember, for example, exactly what you were thinking five minutes ago?

### 3. Storage failure

Sometimes memories are not stored properly or completely and so they become difficult to retrieve from the memory store. This means that sometimes the memory is not there to retrieve at all. If a memory has only been partially stored, it is also harder to retrieve.

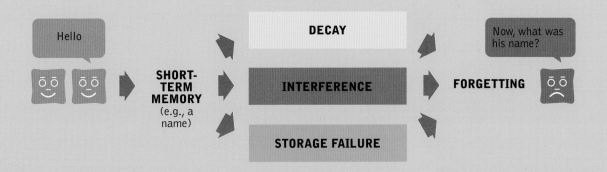

# OTHER FACTORS IN FORGETTING

Memory performance may be affected by many things: How tired you feel, how much coffee you have had, whether you have had a beer, how stressed or calm you feel, or how much is going on around you. Common factors that influence forgetting are:

- **Physical state**: Fatigue, discomfort or pain, arousal level
- **Cognitive factors**: Attention, concentration
- **Emotional factors**: Stress, worry, sadness, elation
- **Environmental factors**: Sounds, smells, light level
- **Task demands**: Easy (boring/mundane) to challenging (complex/taxing)
- **Meta-memory**: Your knowledge of how good or bad your memory is for different things

## REHEARSAL FAILURES AND DISTANT MEMORIES

There are specific reasons why we forget at different stages of memory. We know that, for example, if you don't repeat things in your working memory, the information will disappear or decay. If you were asked to describe a topic you covered in history when you were in school, you would be hard-pressed to do so. It is probably not something you have thought about for a long time, and it is in the very depths of your memory stores. If you started to read a little about the topic, you would find that, little by little, the information would come back, your memory having been refreshed.

### The effects of alcohol

When we drink alcohol, it affects us in many ways. It changes our ability to divide our attention, it affects our visual perception of depth and space, our ability to concentrate, and our judgment. If you're of legal drinking age, try one of the memory tests in Step 3 both before and after a couple of alcoholic drinks. You will be surprised at how much it affects your memory (see also pages 124–127).

# "Who starred in that old movie?"

# "It's on the tip of my tongue."

# ENTRY DENIED
## Factors affecting memory entry and storage

*Let's look first* at how information comes in and what might affect whether it is properly stored or not. One of the biggest problems is the cacophony of sounds, images, emotions, and general hubbub of daily life that are constantly being moved from the brain's sensory store to your working memory. At this very moment, this system is churning away in your brain. You may be thinking about something that happened a few minutes or even a few days ago. It has come up from the sensory register into the conscious mind—the working memory. Your attention, meanwhile, is trying to help you by telling you to concentrate on what you are doing right now.

### EXERCISE

Write a list of seven things going on in your mind right now and things that, if you start to pay attention, you are aware of. Your list might include some of the following:

1. The sound of a plane overhead
2. The thought of how much work you have to do
3. The sound of the TV
4. Computer alerts to incoming emails
5. Urban sounds, like sirens or traffic
6. The feeling of fatigue, since you did not get much sleep last night
7. The feeling of hunger and the half-remembered plan to meet someone for lunch

### Filtering out unimportant information

Now we can see that the mind's eyes and ears are constantly being bombarded with information. Your memory system, however, helps to direct what is important at the moment to your current "thinking" goals (what you are trying to achieve), such as finishing a work assignment. It seems to handle, or filter, external information to allow you to focus and does not allow anything deemed unimportant to enter the memory. If this did not happen, the memory would soon become overloaded.

### Rehearsal and how it can fail

It used to be thought that once you have repeated something over and over (a process known as **rehearsal**), it would set up a memory in long-term storage. Therefore, a cause of forgetting was that a person had not repeated the information enough. Some early research supported this idea: If you had people repeat lists of numbers and words, they would usually remember them later. This method was commonly used in education and was called **learning by rote**. However, you may be aware of having repeatedly looked up a telephone number to dial it and it never stuck in your mind. There is evidence that just repeating something is not usually sufficient or the most effective way of storing memories long-term.

There is a distinction now drawn between **maintenance rehearsal**, for keeping things in working memory, and **encoding rehearsal**, for moving things from working memory into long-term storage. This means that forgetting is probably due to believing you have done enough by repetition and that another, additional, strategy is not needed. But it usually is. When it comes to that last-minute read-through of your exam notes, you are probably more likely to remember the information if you can visualize the order that the facts were written on the sheet. It is even better if you actually understand them or have made up a story around them.

# Repetition isn't the most
## successful memory strategy.

# LACK OF ASSOCIATION

Long-term memory works by storing pieces of meaningful information together, with links to related areas. Although much of what is stored in our long-term memories is naturally organized, sometimes we need to create our own links with a little conscious effort. Often, therefore, when someone says they have forgotten something, it may mean that it has only been partially stored or that it has not been sorted into the right place and is still in the area labeled "miscellaneous." If information isn't stored properly, it will decay.

## Lack of understanding

To remember information well, you need to understand it and give it meaning. A study was carried out with eleven-year-old children. They were asked to remember a passage about boomerangs. One group remembered the passage much more readily than the other. When the investigators asked them what they did, many said that they automatically asked questions about the passage ("What are boomerangs used for?"; "What do they look like?"; "Where are they from?"). The ones who did not remember as well had not asked such questions. Those who asked questions were putting meaning into their associations and were therefore better at remembering the information. They were linking what was new information with what was already in their memory.

| **BOOMERANG** | **AUSTRALIA** | **KANGAROO** |
| (word) | (mental picture) | (familiar associated object) |

# ACCESS DENIED
## Factors affecting retrieval

*When you access* a memory, you are not simply replaying a tape; you are, in fact, re-creating an experience, rewriting a script. So what, then, affects retrieval? The tempting answer is to say everything. All along the pathway of information getting into storage, there are things that may help retrieval to happen, or not.

## DEPTH AND BREADTH OF PROCESSING

There is a generally held view that the more elaborate and better processed information is in the first place, the less likely it is to be forgotten. Notice that the really good memorizers in the school example on page 27 did not just ask "What is a boomerang?" but imagined it ("What does it look like?"). So they processed it both as a visual image and as a meaningful set of words, maybe even with a little rhyme: "The man with the didgeridoo threw the boomerang to a kangaroo." This would have made the information highly accessible for retrieval as it has been given depth and breadth.

If the children were asked a few weeks later to remember the pictures, some might still remember it well—if they had encoded it well with good depth and breadth. But they would probably remember less than on the day it was shown to them and have to do some guesswork ("It was Australia, crocodiles, and a boomerang"). Over time, memories—even in long-term memory—fade and are not easily retrieved.

### Recognition versus recall

Some kinds of memories remain more stable than others. **Recognition memory**—being able to recognize something you have seen before—may be quite reliable but **recalling memory** may not. If you look at a school photograph, you may recognize many of the faces, but find it difficult to retrieve any names. If you were told the first name, however, you would probably remember the last name.

# *Would you recognize your dentist if you saw him in the supermarket?*

## INTERFERENCE

As with encoding, retrieval can be affected by interference. Imagine reading a list of words, then another list of words right afterward. If you were asked the next day to recall the first list of words, you would probably include some from the second list too—because the second list has interfered with your memory of the first list. Information that is very similar—like word lists of common objects—may be more readily mixed up than information that is more distinct.

## CONTEXT AND CUES

One very important factor that affects retrieval of memories is the context you are in. There may well be many cues that are missing in one environment that would have been present in another. Most people will be aware of environmental context. If you see someone you know in a different environment, you may recognize that you know them but not recall who they are. There have also been studies to show that people who were asked to learn information for a test in a room that had a distinctive smell (cinnamon, for example) were better at remembering when tested in a room that had the same smell.

Studies have been carried out showing that if a memory test is completed in a particular context, the information will be recalled much more readily in that particular context. That is why, when you go into a room for something and then can't remember what it was, you will usually remember if you go back where you started.

There are also internal cues. Imagine you have had a few alcoholic drinks and have an interesting chat with someone. You may remember that you had the chat, but you may not remember all of it. Next time you have a drink with the same person you may recall more of what you talked about. Beware, however—too much alcohol causes serious memory loss (see pages 126–127).

# MALES AND FEMALES

*It is apparent* that women and men process information differently. There is no clear explanation for this, but there are three possible reasons.

**1. NATURAL VARIATION** There may be basic biological differences—think of it as slightly different hardware accompanied by slightly different software. For example, it appears from research that the corpus callosum, which connects the two lobes of the brain together, is slightly larger (denser) in women than men. One theoretical interpretation of this is that the right (emotional) and left (rational) sides communicate better.

**2. EARLY CONDITIONING** It may be due to the way that we are treated as children. For example, there is evidence that adults treat children dressed in blue and pink differently. They will implicitly stereotype the child in pink as a girl and tend (without being aware of it) to discourage adventurousness. The one in blue is perceived as a boy, and will have behavior that reflects competition and single-mindedness.

**3. NATURE AND NURTURE** It may be a combination of the above factors.

## WHAT ARE WOMEN GOOD AT?

Women, in general, are better than men at doing certain language tasks, develop language faster, are better at making emotional judgments, and are better at tests involving the generation of ideas.

• **MULTITASKING** Women are usually better than men at doing several things at once, probably because of a better connection between the right and left sides of the brain. Imagine you are a hotel clerk checking a guest in. There is a call you have to deal with at the same time. At that same moment, you are asked by another guest to pass on a message. Research shows that women are better than men at passing on the message.

- **AUTOBIOGRAPHICAL MEMORY** Women appear to be better at remembering things from the past, particularly emotional episodes.

# WHAT ARE MEN GOOD AT?

Men generally outperform women in mathematical reasoning tasks, score higher on tests that distinguish figure from background, find it easier to rotate objects in their mind's eye, have more accurate aim, and are better at remembering technical information. This is probably due to one area of the brain being dominant at any one time. They are naturally more sequential in processing, but generally they are not able to be as emotionally connected.

## Memory during pregnancy

Short-term memory appears to change in women during pregnancy. This may be contributed to by poorer concentration (caused by a preoccupation with the impending new arrival, sickness, and fatigue) and changes in hormone levels. Recent studies have shown that memory changes are most likely to be perceived and not real and lasting. Many changes appear to be due to life-change factors, including fatigue, weight gain, altered appearance, and lack of interest in sex.

Another explanation is the high level of oxytocin, a chemical known to impair memory, which is produced in the body during the third trimester. Another possibility is the increase in free cortisol levels during the third trimester. There is evidence that high levels of cortisol affect the hippocampus, which plays a crucial role in memory. It may well be a combination of these psychological, hormonal, and chemical factors.

# MEMORY
# BLOCKS

*For various reasons*, memories sometimes become "blocked." Sometimes they still exist in the mind, but accessing them is impossible. In other cases, the storing of the memories has been prevented in the first place.

## REPRESSED MEMORIES

Sometimes memories may be so emotional or unpleasant that they become too difficult to recall. According to psychoanalytic theory, developed by such people as Sigmund Freud (1856–1939), one reason for forgetting something is that a memory is in fact not forgotten, but repressed. It is there at some level, but the person has repressed it because it is too painful to be consciously aware of. This is a controversial area of research. There have been a number of cases where therapists have gotten patients to "unblock" the fact that they were sexually abused as a child. It is not clear, however, whether this is a real memory or a suggested memory.

## TRAUMA

It may be that a memory has not been lost or repressed, rather that it is very difficult to actually put into words. Research with survivors of traumatic events has shown that it is common for many not to remember—consciously—some of what happened, but they may still have memories that can be triggered by cues other than words, such as sound, smell, or touch. For example, the sound of a siren may trigger a feeling of anxiety in someone who has been in an accident, or they may have very vivid dreams reliving the event. This is commonly known as **post-traumatic stress disorder**. In this syndrome, one type of therapy is to get the patient to talk about the accident, to try to put it into words and release the anxiety associated with it.

# *Relax, smile, and remember.*

## STRESS

Stress plays a big role in forgetting, since when people are stressed, they find it harder to take in information, probably because their working memory is filled with all kinds of negative thoughts, which take up valuable processing space. Some degree of mental arousal stress (positive stress) is important to motivation, but if it becomes too much, then working memory can be overwhelmed and the memory system paralyzed. For example, when you are overwhelmed with simply far too much to do.

## DEPRESSION

Suffering from depression is another significant cause of memory problems, both taking in new memories and recalling existing ones. Even relatively mild depression can cause a poor psychological state. For example, frustration, worry, or perhaps preoccupation with sad or negative thoughts can significantly affect a person's concentration and memory. Depression also causes changes in specific chemical systems in the brain involved with mood and memory, such as serotonin.

## MEDICATION

Some types of medication can cause memory difficulties. This is a common side-effect, for example, with sleeping pills. Different medications may also interact badly to cause changes in memory function.

IN → **MEMORY FORMATION BLOCKS:** stress, depression, medication → **MEMORY STORES** → **MEMORY RETRIEVAL BLOCKS:** repression, trauma → OUT

# AGE
# AND MEMORY

*Memory changes* with age, largely due to stages of brain development. What is fascinating is that the last area of the brain to develop fully (the frontal lobes) is the first part that starts to deteriorate with age.

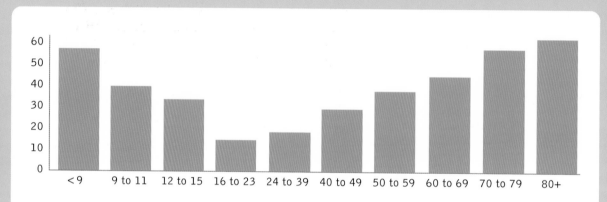

This graph shows the typical pattern across the age span. The bars show the number of errors on a memory test. You can see that young children make approximately the same number of memory errors as older people. Our memory is at its optimum between the ages of sixteen to twenty-three years, and from then on it gradually deteriorates.

## CHILDHOOD AMNESIA

It is rare to remember anything from when you were a very small child. This is because the brain is not fully formed in children under four years. A child's temporal lobes develop first, and these are responsible for remembering patterns (such as faces). The frontal lobes develop last, and so working memories are the last thing to develop. In addition, we don't acquire language fully until past the age of two years, and language is likely to be a crucial factor in memory.

Young children make many memory errors in formal tests. A child's perception of the world is not yet developed, and so it is difficult for them to make associations. The memories may be there, but the child may not be able to access them. The exception tends to be if a significant event affects a child. The memory may then be present. However, it may have also become a memory through the child's parents telling them about it when they are older, so they have almost made it into a "story."

## Imaginary friends

Many children have imaginary friends. One theory is that they are learning about their memory. Memory is a collection of stories about us, and as we age, we understand that there are lots of reasons for them. They give us a personal history, they help us to understand things, and they are important to our everyday functioning. Children don't usually understand this. They even have difficulty understanding the distinction between imaginary and real. Have you ever been unsure whether you experienced something or dreamed it? This is probably what it is like for children.

## THE IMPACT OF INCREASING AGE

Most people notice a change in their memory as they get older. It is natural that just as our bodies start to falter so do our brains, and this particularly affects our short-term memory. You can see from the graph that older adults make more memory errors than younger adults. They tend to become worse at working memory and recall first, because the frontal lobes are the first part of the brain to deteriorate. Physical factors can also play a part. Reduced hearing and vision can affect your memory function, since they are barriers to being able to take information in effectively and efficiently.

Our strategy-generation system also becomes less efficient as we age. However, research has shown that if older individuals are taught a strategy, they can then use it quite effectively.

## USE IT OR LOSE IT

There is a theory that if you exercise your brain after retirement by doing puzzles and crosswords, pursuing hobbies, joining book clubs, and so on, you may protect your memory from changing too much. This is called the **use it or lose it** theory (see also pages 112–113).

# SELF-ASSESSMENT

**What are your strengths and weaknesses?** *Are you organized? Is your lifestyle reducing your optimum level of functioning? Are you better at remembering visually or verbally? Is your memory good for facts? Over the next two steps, you will build up a better picture of yourself by completing a number of exercises. To understand how you can improve your memory, it is first necessary to assess yourself with regard to your everyday memory, your general approach to life, and your motivation and goals. Only when you have a clear picture of where you are now, will you be able to start moving toward where you would like to be.*

## Important facts about memory

Memory varies according to:
- Sex
- Age

Factors that affect memory include:
- Poor concentration
- Stress
- Poor psychological state

Memory is:
- Active
- Complex

There are three basic memory processes:
- Encoding
- Storage
- Retrieval

There are different subtypes of memory:
- Semantic
- Episodic

## YOUR EVERYDAY MEMORY

No doubt you will have experienced memory difficulties that make you think you are particularly bad at certain types of information. You may also be aware of particular situations where you find your memory is worse. No one has a perfect memory, and most people probably don't have a better memory than you. By now, you will be aware that we all have different strengths and weaknesses, and different factors affect our memory performance—such as how well we are concentrating, how tired or stressed we are, hormones, alcohol, or medication. Other factors such as age are also important, because as we get older, our brains age, just like our bodies.

There is also natural variation in our basic memory abilities, even from week to week, depending on what is going on in our lives. This is why sometimes you may feel that you are remembering better and are sharper than at other times. You will notice, for example, that having a hangover seems to make complex tasks and recall much more difficult. Natural variations in hormone levels, for example, have a similar effect, and we have little control over this.

## OTHER PEOPLE'S MEMORY

Comparing yourself to others is rarely helpful. Memory is linked to intelligence, but more often than not, when you think that someone else seems to have a much better memory than you do, it is often that you are simply seeing one of their areas of strength, which is perhaps a weaker area for you. Alternatively, if in a business situation, you are impressed by how well your boss always seems to be able to remember clients' names, it is more than likely that she is using a memory strategy. Although there is probably nothing wrong with your memory, there are always ways to improve or optimize it.

# FACTORS
## AFFECTING MEMORY

## CONFIDENCE

Very often, we are our own self-fulfilling prophecies, only achieving as much as we think we can. In fact, it is frequently the case that people may appear to be more intelligent, or to have a better memory, simply because they believe in themselves and have confidence.

There is a perception, for example, that people who go to college must be superbright. While, of course, this may be true, in many cases, students achieve good exam results and go to college because they have worked hard and gained confidence through their accomplishments. Often such individuals have had the good fortune to attend good schools with excellent teachers, where they have been able to learn a lot and to have confidence in themselves.

Others may not have been so lucky—perhaps they attended schools where excelling was seen as "uncool," or were told that they were average. They may have had little opportunity to study after school due to poor facilities at home, and would not even have considered applying to college. So, learn to believe in yourself and have confidence in your own abilities. Make a list of the things that you are able to do—you may be surprised at how long it is!

## STRESS

This is an important factor in memory function (see also pages 128–129). It is one of the key issues in "poor" memory, as it causes our brains to "freeze." Try to relax and you will be surprised at how much your memory improves.

# *Be a tortoise, not a hare.*

## ILLNESS

Disease can also seriously affect your memory—not feeling your best is very distracting. More serious brain disorders (such as bipolar disorder, depression, schizophrenia, Parkinson's disease, Alzheimer's disease, hydrocephalus, and many others) and brain damage affect the physical and chemical order in your brain and have an adverse effect on your memory and concentration.

In such situations, it is advisable to seek medical advice, to have a formal assessment of your memory function, and to undergo specific rehabilitation training to help you to improve in your less than optimal areas. You can also help yourself by gaining a greater understanding of your memory strengths and weaknesses, and by learning how to get around your difficulties by using internal and external strategies.

## TEMPERAMENT AND PERSONALITY TYPE

We all have different personalities, and there is a broad range of types. One extreme is the fast-thinking extrovert. Quick thinking can be useful, but this can also be the type of person who doesn't listen properly, makes mistakes, doesn't think before they speak, and has poor concentration. This type of person also tends to have a less healthy lifestyle, to be less organized, and to try to fit too much in.

By contrast, at the other end of the spectrum are the introverted types who appear to be slower and much quieter—the "plodders." Yet such individuals can often be the ones who listen carefully, are more methodical and organized, and concentrate better.

# EXERCISE 1: YOUR GENERAL APPROACH TO LIFE

*This questionnaire* consists of twenty groups of statements. Please read each group of statements carefully and then pick out the one statement that best describes how you feel about yourself now. Circle the number beside the statement that you have picked. If more than one statement in the group seems to apply, circle the highest number for that group. Don't choose more than one statement for any group.

**How organized do you consider yourself to be?**
1. Not at all
2. Reasonably organized
3. Very organized

**When you are in a meeting, which statement best suits you?**
1. I find myself drifting off and thinking about other things.
2. I can take information in well, but only if the subject is interesting.
3. I can concentrate with no difficulty and remember well at all times.

**Do you mislay your keys?**
1. Often
2. Sometimes
3. Never

**Do you keep an appointments calendar?**
1. No
2. I try to, but find it difficult to keep it up to date.
3. Yes

**Do you have a hangover more than once a week?**
1. Yes
2. Sometimes
3. No

## Do you find that you constantly have too much to do?

1. Yes, I am not very good at keeping on top of things.
2. I sometimes have to work late to keep up.
3. No, I am reasonably on top of things.

## Do you have difficulty recalling passwords?

1. Yes, I have difficulty remembering such things.
2. I occasionally have some problems recalling them—I use different ones for different occasions.
3. No, I use familiar ones that are easy to remember.

## Do you ever go into a room and forget what you went in for?

1. Often
2. Sometimes
3. Never

## Do you eat plenty of fresh vegetables and fruit?

1. No
2. I try to
3. Yes

## Do you remember to send people birthday cards?

1. No, I don't make a note of dates and so don't know when to send them.
2. Only to people close to me
3. Yes, I keep a list of birthdays.

## Are you easily distracted?

1. Yes, I find it hard to keep my mind focused on one thing for very long.
2. Sometimes
3. Never

## Do you find it easy to take in new information?

1. No
2. When I listen carefully
3. Yes

## Do you keep your mind active?

1. Not really
2. I try to
3. Yes

## Do you doodle?

1. Often
2. Sometimes
3. Never

## Are your household bills organized?

1. No
2. In reasonable order
3. Yes, I organize as I go along so that I am always up to date

## How often do you exercise?

1. Never, I hate exercise.
2. Sometimes
3. At least twice a week

## Do you lose things?

1. Often
2. Sometimes
3. Never

## When you are introduced to someone new, can you remember his/her name?

1. Hardly ever
2. Sometimes
3. Every time

## Do you daydream?

1. Often
2. Sometimes
3. Hardly ever

## Do you get stressed about things?

1. Often
2. Sometimes
3. Hardly ever

**ADD UP YOUR TOTAL SCORE AND SEE WHAT SORT OF MEMORY PERSONALITY YOU HAVE.**

# Scoring

## SCORE 20–30: POOR OPTIMIZER

You probably don't concentrate very well and may feel that you don't have a very good memory. You are likely to be disorganized. You tend not to actively use memory strategies or memory aids, such as making lists. You may not have a particularly healthy lifestyle.

If you have this personality type, there are many things that you can do to improve your everyday memory function by learning how to improve your concentration and using memory strategies. Being able to concentrate is essential for taking information in and storing it. Memory strategies or memory aids can help you store memory information better. You may also need to consider improving your lifestyle habits, because health can have a serious impact on your memory.

## SCORE 31–45: AVERAGE OPTIMIZER

You probably manage reasonably well in life, but feel that you could remember better. You are probably fairly organized, but there is room for improvement. You make an attempt to live a healthy lifestyle, but you are not always successful—you feel that you are too busy.

Becoming more organized, learning to use memory strategies more efficiently, and learning new strategies will greatly improve your memory and concentration. Lifestyle improvements should also be part of your overall improvement plan.

## SCORE 46–60: GOOD OPTIMIZER

You are likely already to have a good memory and to use memory strategies effectively. You are also likely to strive for a healthy lifestyle and have relatively low stress levels.

There is still room for improvement—if you were to learn more about your memory by becoming more aware of how it works and learning new strategies, you could empower your memory even more.

# MOTIVATION
## AND GOALS

*In response to* the question *"What makes people happy?" Sigmund Freud is reported to have said "work and love." This is a good theory, for which there is support. It seems that work—even though we may often wish to be rid of it— provides much-needed purpose and structure in many people's lives. Love and play also help us meet our basic human needs.*

## NEEDS AND GOALS

One system for thinking about needs, goals, and motivation comes from the work of the American psychologist Abraham Maslow (1908–70). He developed, with colleagues, a way of thinking about what people want to achieve and why. The main goal of human activity, he believed, was self-actualization—achieving a realization of one's dreams and capabilities. Maslow described five levels of needs in a hierarchy that people satisfy on the route to self-actualization.

The five levels of needs in the table below lead to people formulating goals that are related to their means for meeting such needs.

| | |
|---|---|
| 1. Physiological needs | Minimal essentials of life—food, shelter, and so on. |
| 2. Safety needs | Protection from dangers in the environment. |
| 3. Attachment needs | To feel a sense of belonging and love. |
| 4. Esteem needs | To feel competent and respected by others and by oneself. |
| 5. Self-actualization needs | To feel creative and explorative, and to have a sense of connection with the world. |

# *Think about what will make you happy.*

## Example

Katy is a twenty-eight-year-old software designer with a college degree and good prospects. Her overall goal in life is to be happy and have a lifestyle where she gets an overall sense of fulfillment from the balance between her relationships, work, play, and sense of commitment. To start with, she broke this down into three smaller goals.

### Goal 1

To maintain a good job so that there are resources for living.
- Needs: An apartment, a car, good food.
- Solution: She worked hard at her job and strove for success.

### Goal 2

To have an active social life.
- Needs: To see her friends, perhaps to meet a partner, to relax.
- Solution: She arranged regular evenings out, doing things that she and her friends enjoyed in a sociable environment.

### Goal 3

To be involved in voluntary work for an environmental group to help stop sea pollution.
- Needs: To feel safe because she swims regularly in the sea, to prevent turtles and coral reefs dying as a result of pollution.
- Solution: She designed and ran a web page for the environmental group.

# Setting personal goals

In the previous example, Katy may have gotten to a point in her life where she felt she had a good balance of work, play, love, and, indeed, self-actualization. Implicitly (and sometimes explicitly), people set goals for themselves. If we don't set our own goals, these may be set for us by others and by society. For example, some students may say that they don't really know why they are studying and have no plans for the future. Others, like Katy, may say that they are studying so they can look for a good job to earn enough money for a reasonable standard of living. Setting goals is important so that you can identify what you want to achieve and what you need to do to achieve it.

### Example

Katy needed more specific goals, especially to do with improving her memory. She wanted to get better at remembering names, planning ahead, and working out routes. This was because she has a poor sense of direction and was often late for appointments, which meant that she was late arriving at work and late getting home. She was also worried that she was starting to be seen as unreliable because she did not always get jobs done on time. She thought this might damage her promotion prospects. Sometimes when she was socializing, she became embarrassed because she couldn't easily remember people's names.

**To improve further, she followed these simple steps:**
- She kept a diary and did tests in order to understand her weaknesses.
- She set herself some specific goals to achieve regarding her weak areas (for example, getting at least 60 percent of jobs done on time, and arriving punctually at least 80 percent of the time).
- She set a time frame to achieve the goals.

**She also addressed the following questions:**
- What skills or abilities must be developed in order to achieve the goals?
- In what place(s) will it be possible to achieve the goals?
- What resources are needed to achieve the goals?

For Katy to achieve her goals, she needed to make sure she knew the time frame, what skills she could learn (and learn them), where she needed to be (and how to get there), and what resources she needed. She started to develop strategies to help her with names and directions. She was explicit about what her goals were and specific about what that meant, and then organized what action she needed to take.

| think | specific goals | time frame | set of actions |

# Setting your own memory goals

Think first about why you want to improve your memory. You may say that it is because you want a better memory. But is that all? Furthermore, how would you know when it was better? Setting goals will help to make sure you know:

- **What you are working toward**
- **Why you are motivated toward it**
- **Whether you have achieved it**

## Keep a diary

Start off by keeping a memory and lifestyle diary for one week (see also page 68). Note the following:

- What sorts of things you regularly forget
- How often you find yourself losing concentration or not listening
- What types of events make you start to feel stressed out
- How many alcoholic drinks you have each day
- How late you stay up each night
- How often you achieve what you want to each day

## Draw up a chart

A chart can help you establish what your memory goals are, and also help you achieve them by keeping track of how you are doing. Here is an example:

| Goal | Method | May 1 | June 1 | July 1 |
|------|--------|-------|--------|--------|
| Remembering names | Using strategies | Improving | Improving | |
| Keeping appointments | Better organization, planning | Improving | Much better | |
| Not losing keys | Always put in the same place | Achieved! | | |

# YOUR PERSONAL MEMORY PROFILE

*In Step 4 you will be able to learn more about your own memory profile by completing different exercises and then plotting your scores to understand your own personal strengths and weaknesses. At the end of the section, you will be able to fill in a chart that will show where your strengths and weaknesses lie. The rest of the book will demonstrate how you can improve your memory. A greater awareness of your weaker areas can lead you to try out different methods to find strategies that suit you personally.*

## AREAS OF ASSESSMENT

Following on from Exercise 1, which you completed in the previous step, you will be presented with a series of tasks to assess the following different types of memory:

- short-term memory
- long-term memory
- verbal memory
- visual memory
- memory for facts
- memory for your life
- memory for the future

## *Where are your weaknesses?*

# EXERCISE 2: ASSESSING YOUR SHORT-TERM MEMORY

## Part 1: Assessing your memory for numbers

Ask a friend to read out the following sequences of numbers, starting with just two numbers and progressing to twelve. Don't look at the numbers. Your task is to repeat the same numbers back in the same order. Go as far as you can.

| | | | | | | | | | | | |
|---|---|---|---|---|---|---|---|---|---|---|---|
| 45 | 12 | | | | | | | | | | |
| 6 | 10 | 34 | | | | | | | | | |
| 17 | 99 | 83 | 5 | | | | | | | | |
| 3 | 68 | 24 | 37 | 12 | | | | | | | |
| 19 | 21 | 67 | 82 | 15 | 16 | | | | | | |
| 78 | 55 | 87 | 90 | 23 | 45 | 79 | | | | | |
| 54 | 7 | 2 | 18 | 48 | 81 | 96 | 33 | | | | |
| 11 | 52 | 3 | 89 | 44 | 67 | 28 | 1 | 92 | | | |
| 77 | 46 | 38 | 16 | 8 | 10 | 24 | 26 | 31 | 66 | | |
| 92 | 6 | 4 | 71 | 85 | 56 | 78 | 94 | 30 | 40 | 13 | |
| 67 | 14 | 49 | 46 | 59 | 83 | 12 | 9 | 37 | 93 | 20 | 26 |

## Scoring

Your score is how many numbers you were able to recall in one try.
Less than 5 = poor; 5–9 = average; more than 9 = good.

## Summary

Most of us remember an average of seven pieces of information.

## Part 2: **Assessing your memory for word lists (verbal memory)**

Look at the following list of words and try to remember them—don't write the words down. You have one minute. Make sure you have pen and paper handy.

| | | | |
|---|---|---|---|
| DOLL | TRAIN | JACKET | RUG |
| CAR | FOOTBALL | CHAIR | PANTS |
| TABLE | MOTORCYCLE | PUZZLE | SOFA |
| HAT | MARBLES | HELICOPTER | SOCK |

Now cover up the words (don't cheat!) and write down as many of the words as you can.

## Scoring

How many did you remember? Score 1 point for each item you recalled correctly (total 16).
Less than 5 = poor; 5–9 = average; more than 9 = good.

## Summary

Again, you are likely to have remembered between five and nine items. Did you notice any pattern in the words? If not, look again. If you look closely, you will see that the words can be divided into four main categories (toys, transportation, furniture, clothing). One of the easiest ways of improving memory is to group items together in categories. This reduces the memory load, making remembering easier.

## Part 3:  **Assessing your visual and spatial memory**

Look at the following street scene for one minute. Then turn the page
and look at the questions on the next page, marking your answers on a
piece of paper. The answers are on page 52.

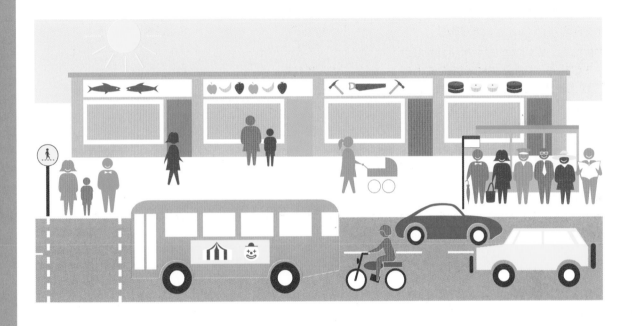

# *Is your visual memory better than*
# *your verbal memory?*

1. How many people were in the line for the bus?
2. What was the man with the bow tie carrying?
3. What color was the sports car?
4. What was advertised on the bus?
5. What was the third store from the left selling?
6. Why had the traffic stopped?
7. What was the last person in the bus line holding?
8. How many stores were there?
9. What was directly behind the bus?
10. What was the weather like?
11. What was the store on the right selling?

## Scoring

How answers did you get right?
Less than 5 = poor; 6–9 = average; 10–12 = good.

## Learning by repetition

See how much you can improve your memory by learning. Repeat the task and see if you can improve on your original score. If you do the test for a third time, you may find that you improve even more.

## ANSWERS:

1. six 2. an umbrella 3. blue 4. a circus 5. hardware 6. People were waiting to cross the road at the crosswalk. 7. a newspaper 8. four 9. a person on a bicycle 10. sunny 11. cake

## Part 4: **Remembering stories**

Read the following paragraph. Don't make notes, but have a pen and paper handy for later.

Michael Robinson was on his way to the local convenience store to buy a newspaper, a carton of eggs, and some jam for his breakfast. On his way home, as he was walking along the sidewalk, he saw a lady trip over a stone and fall to the ground, hitting her head. He ran over to see if she needed help and saw that she had blood coming out of a wound in her head. He ran to the nearest house, knocked on the door, told the woman who answered what had happened, and asked her to telephone for help. After fifteen minutes, an ambulance arrived and took the injured woman to the hospital.

Now cover the paragraph and write down as much of the story as you can remember (as close to the actual words as possible).

## Scoring

How many pieces of information (out of a total of 27) did you recall?
Less than 15 = poor; 16–25 = average; more than 25 = good.

## Summary

Most people will certainly remember the gist of the story and probably some detail, but it is very difficult to remember such a story word for word. How close were you? Our memories are not like recordings. They don't need to be. You may even have found that you fill in bits that you can't remember, as our memories tend to do this.

When we are reading books and newspapers, most of us tend to remember the gist rather than the precise wording. This is because, although the words are important, our memory span is limited; so words become a "route" for a story, and hence we remember only the gist. Luckily, what is important is, of course, what the words convey and not necessarily the words themselves. We are also much better at remembering memorable passages or ones that have personal relevance to us.

## Part 5: **Recognition memory**

All of the tasks so far in this section have been about recalling information. Let's now turn to your recognition memory. Look at these words and make a note of which ones were in the list in Part 2 above. Don't cheat by looking back. Can you recognize which ones you have seen before?

| DOLL | FOOTBALL | TRASH CAN | IRON |
|------|----------|-----------|------|
| CAR | HAT | MOPED | TRAIN |
| MOTORCYCLE | HOUSE | JACKET | HELICOPTER |
| RUG | SOFA | PUZZLE | WINDOW |

## Scoring

Check back and work out your score. You have seen eleven of these words previously. Recognizing less than 9 = poor; 9 = average; 10–11 = good.

## Summary

Most of us are very good at recognizing words. Recognition tends to act as a natural memory prompt, since the words are all there and you just have to distinguish between which ones you have seen and which ones you have not seen. It requires less effort than recall. A quirk of our memory systems is that even though it is easier to recall common items that may come from the same category, it is easier to recognize less common items. The more similar or common items are, the harder it is to distinguish between them.

## *Did you get a feeling of déjà vu?*

# Part 6: **Assessing your visual recognition memory**

Look at the following group of people. Which of them have you seen before? Write down the numbers of the ones you have seen before and then refer to the key below to see how many you got right. You may be surprised at how many you are able to remember.

## ANSWER:

Numbers 1, 3, 6, 7, 8, and 11 are new; the rest appear in the street scene on page 51.

# EXERCISE 3: ASSESSING YOUR LONG-TERM MEMORY

## Part 1: **Episodic memory**

This type of memory tends to fall into different categories.
Try to answer these questions:

1. What did you have for breakfast this morning?
2. What did you do last weekend?
3. What did you do last Wednesday?
4. Where were you when you had your first kiss?
5. Where did you celebrate the turn of the new millennium?
6. What was the last film you watched?
7. Where were you when you heard that Diana, Princess of Wales, had died?
8. What did you do on your last birthday?
9. What was the last TV program you watched?
10. What was the last book you read?

## Scoring

Score 1 point for each episode you could recall.
Under 7 items = poor; 7 items = average; over 7 = good.

### Summary

You probably found some of the above were easier to remember than others. It is much easier to remember where you were or what you were doing when there is an important event or when the event has more personal meaning to you. This is because we don't need to remember every moment of our lives. Our memories naturally sift information and we forget what we don't need to know.

## Part 2: **Semantic memory**

How good is your general knowledge? Semantic memory is our own personal memory for facts. Try to answer the following questions, and see how good your factual knowledge is.

1.   What is the capital of Italy?
2.   Who wrote *A Midsummer Night's Dream*?
3.   In which direction does the sun set?
4.   At what temperature does water boil?
5.   Which planet is fifth furthest from the sun?
6.   In which year was Nelson Mandela freed?
7.   In which year was the Russian Revolution?
8.   How many players are there in a soccer team?
9.   On which continent is Guyana?
10.  In which part of the human body would you find the cornea?
11.  Who was the first explorer to reach the North Pole?
12.  Who wrote *The Origin of Species*?
13.  Which two major oceans border South America?
14.  What is the capital of Belgium?
15.  Where is the Sea of Tranquillity?
16.  What were the dates of the First World War?
17.  Which U.S. President was involved in the Watergate scandal?
18.  Where was Napoleon Bonaparte exiled?
19.  What are the seven colors of the rainbow?
20.  Who played the female lead in *Some Like it Hot*?

## Scoring

Under 10 correct answers = poor; 11–15 = average; 16–20 = good.

The answers are given on page 61, but if you were to look them up for yourself in books or on the Internet, you would be more likely to remember them in the future.

## Summary

Our semantic knowledge varies according to many different factors, including where you are from, what age you are, your interests, and so on. It is easier to extend your semantic knowledge in areas that you already know about, since the knowledge will be more meaningful.

# EXERCISE 4: ASSESSING YOUR PROSPECTIVE MEMORY

*Most of us lead busy lives.* *How often do you forget each of the following?*

**To pay bills (or whether you have paid them or not)**
1. Often
2. Sometimes
3. Never

**What time an appointment is scheduled for**
1. Often
2. Sometimes
3. Never

**To record a television show you will miss because you will be out**
1. Often
2. Sometimes
3. Never

**What your plans are for the following week**
1. Often
2. Sometimes
3. Never

**To cancel the newspapers before going on vacation**
1. Often
2. Sometimes
3. Never

## To draw money out of the ATM before going out
1. Often
2. Sometimes
3. Never

## To set the alarm clock before going to bed
1. Often
2. Sometimes
3. Never

## To take your medications
1. Often
2. Sometimes
3. Never

## To send a birthday card to a good friend
1. Often
2. Sometimes
3. Never

## To return a phone call
1. Often
2. Sometimes
3. Never

## Scoring
Add up your scores.
10–15 = poor; 16–25 = average; 26–30 = good.

## Summary
We are all guilty of forgetting to do things from time to time, and it can be very frustrating when we forget. The good thing about this type of memory is that it is very easy to improve. With a little organization and the aid of simple strategies, you will find that you can improve this area of memory. Sometimes it seems as though our lives are taken up by lots of little tasks. Getting organized can help to clear your mind so that you can get on with more interesting things.

# YOUR PERSONAL PROFILE

So how did you perform overall?
To find out, check off the relevant boxes in the following chart.

| Exercise no. | Type of test | Poor | Average | Good |
|---|---|---|---|---|
| 1 | General approach | | | |
| 2 (part 1) | Number memory | | | |
| 2 (part 2) | Verbal memory | | | |
| 2 (part 3) | Visual/spatial memory | | | |
| 2 (part 4) | Story memory | | | |
| 2 (part 5) | Recognition memory | | | |
| 2 (part 6) | Visual recognition memory | | | |
| 3 (part 1) | Episodic memory | | | |
| 3 (part 2) | Semantic memory | | | |
| 4 | Prospective memory | | | |

# INTERPRETING YOUR PERSONAL STRENGTHS AND WEAKNESSES

Have a look at how you scored on each different exercise. It should now be clear in which areas you are strongest and weakest. It is natural that you will have some stronger areas than others, because we all have different memory strengths and weaknesses. There are many things you can do to improve. Becoming more organized and using different strategies will help you. Even if you have scored highly in every area, you may still be able to improve your memory.

## Answers to quiz on page 57

1. Rome 2. William Shakespeare 3. The west 4. 212°F 5. Jupiter 6. 1990 7. 1917 8. Eleven 9. South America 10. The eye 11. Robert Edwin Peary 12. Charles Darwin 13. Pacific and Atlantic 14. Brussels 15. On the moon 16. 1914–1918 17. Richard Nixon 18. St Helena 19. Red, orange, yellow, green, blue, indigo, violet 20. Marilyn Monroe

# CRITICAL
# THINKING SKILLS

*Because memory is complex* and multifaceted, it is important to try to understand how other relevant mental functions are involved with memory and why they are so important to memory. Concentration is an essential part of memory, but so are the processes of planning, organizing, and effective learning. This step guides you through these skills in order to help you improve your memory. First, however, you must make sure that you are fully aware of your own capabilities.

## Knowing your own memory

This is the ability to recognize whether we know something or remember something, because we know we have the information in our memory. It is also known as **meta-memory**. It helps us to monitor whether we know information or not—that aspect of memory function that allows us to know that we know something. Completing the personal memory profile in Step 3 will help you discover what your strengths and weaknesses are, so that you know what aspects to concentrate on. Once you start to have adequate knowledge of your own personal strengths and weaknesses, you can learn how these can help to influence and improve your memory in different situations.

*Do you know how much you know?*

## Using simple strategies

This basic understanding can help you use appropriate, timely strategies when necessary. Here are some examples.

- If you know that you are bad at remembering names, in situations where you are introduced to new people, be ready to listen carefully and try to use strategies to process the name better. For example, when introduced to new people, pick out something visually memorable and relate it to their name: Robert in red, Barbara in a blouse, and so on.

- If you are studying for an exam but you know that your concentration is not so good at the end of the day, get up early and study in the morning when your concentration is better.

- If you know that your boss does not like to be disturbed in the morning, make an appointment to see him or her after lunch.

  Increased awareness of our own memory strengths and shortfalls, coupled with strategies like the ones above, can help us improve our memories.

# THE POWER
## OF CONCENTRATION

*Concentration allows us* to attend to information so that it stays around long enough to be useful. It involves a state of mental alertness, concentrating over time, resisting distraction, and efficiently dividing resources between different demands. Poor concentration means that information does not get taken in, and memories then have no chance of getting into our long-term stores. It is very often the case that memory loss, or apparently "poor memory," is simply a failure to pay enough attention in the first place. It is obvious really, but you must not underestimate its importance. It is easy to sharpen your memory when you realize this simple fact: Paying attention is crucial to memory processing.

## ATTENTION SKILLS

Most of us lead very busy lives, with far too much to do. It is hardly surprising that, with so much going on, we can be poor at concentrating on the important things. So the ability to identify important ideas, details, names, and so on is critical to the effective recall of information. We have a system that has evolved to help us pay attention (or not) to things. There are different kinds of attention skills that help your short-term working memory to process information.

### Sustained attention

This refers to our ability to continue to concentrate on something for a sustained period of time. Motivation and mental arousal level are key factors affecting attention. To sustain your attention long enough to process information into memory (that is, to encode it), you need to keep a good balance between being stimulated and overstimulated. You also need to be mindful that you have a window of sustainable attention—twenty minutes, forty minutes, maybe a bit longer—depending on the type of information you are processing.

# Example

- Imagine you are working on your computer at the office and in the background is a financial program on TV giving information about stocks. There is too much on the screen to take all of it in—a business bar, sets of figures, a presenter talking. You may pay just enough attention to the program to know that, in general, the market is reasonable at the moment.

- Imagine, now, that you suddenly hear that one particular sector of the market (the fashion industry) is not doing so well because one of the major fashion houses has gone bust. Your attention is caught because you have some shares in a fashion house called Glamco. You look and listen for any information on those shares. Your attention is sustained for much of the program in case Glamco is mentioned. After a little while, the presenter starts to talk about Glamco. After the end of the program, you turn your attention back to your work and ignore the television.

- Imagine, finally, that you plan to sell your Glamco shares on the Internet, but your computer has crashed. You are listening to instructions from your computer-support service. You may focus on these instructions quite well, but if you are getting really anxious, there may be an overload of alertness. You may have gone past your optimum level of mental arousal, and the instructions may be mangled in your mind. In fact, you may have so many worrisome thoughts that there is not enough space in your working memory for the instructions.

### Divided attention

What competes with the ability to sustain attention on one thing is all those other things that want to take your interest. Sometimes you may need to consciously keep two or more things in mind at the same time. This is known as **divided attention** (or **dual attention** when it is only two things). Usually, you will switch according to **selective attention**. That is, you may pay attention to what is more important, bearing the other in mind and switching to it when it becomes more important. This is the essential underlying skill for multitasking.

## Example

Imagine yourself at your desk working again. You are trying to finish a set of accounts. At the same time, you want to check how the Glamco shares are doing, because, after the market news, they are fluctuating and you are deciding whether to sell or not. Your desk is in an open-plan office. There is a hubbub as one team has just been told it is underperforming and must improve. Your phone rings—a customer wants to find out some information. While you are talking to her, you once again check your online share account for the Glamco shares. You finish the phone call and turn back to your work. You smell coffee brewing and gesture that you would like one, too. A colleague asks you if you are going to the interoffice softball challenge. Again you check the Glamco shares.

In the previous example, there were many demands on your attention, but you still managed effectively. This is because the brain's natural attention system helped you to focus on what you needed for the immediate and next job in hand. If there are too many data streams, then you will be overwhelmed, and if you are multitasking, you may find you make mistakes. Some people are good at divided attention and can deal with the multiple loads; others are more serial, that is, better at handling one thing at a time. It is also easier to divide attention when some of the tasks you are doing are very familiar.

### Driving a car

The art of driving a car is what is called a **procedural skill**. You probably took a while to learn, but since you passed your test and have had some practice, you now drive without even thinking about it. This is because it is such a well-learned skill that it becomes automatic. Automatic memory is one of the deepest memories we have, and automatic memories are very difficult to forget. So, even if you did not drive for ten years, you would still be able to get into a car and drive. We can even do other things while we are driving—talk to a passenger, watch out for pedestrians crossing the road, sip from a bottle of water, or adjust the radio. We can divide our attention easily since we are carrying out a very familiar memory procedure.

# *Driving is complicated, but memory makes it easy.*

# ORGANIZATION
## AND PLANNING AHEAD

*Being organized is a crucial* component of memory. People often say "you must have a system." The more structured your system is (and getting organized can take practice), the better you will find your memory—particularly your prospective memory (that is, remembering to do things like pay bills). Organizing yourself will also reduce stress in your life, and when you are on top of things, you will naturally relax and find that you have better recall and are better at taking in new information. Obviously, we all have to account for everyday interruptions, and at times we may even have to cope with emergency situations. On the whole, however, planning can seriously help you improve your memory and your quality of life.

### Time management

This is an effective way of improving your planning and organization and, as a result, enhancing your memory performance. Many of you will have heard of this concept, but what does it actually mean? The answer is creating a system through which you can effectively cope with and enjoy both your work and your personal life. We all have different ways of doing things, different obligations, and so on, and no plan can be prescribed, but there are basic principles that you can apply:

- **Draw up a life plan.**
- **Use an electronic organizer.**
- **Get things done.**
- **Delegate tasks.**
- **Make lists.**
- **Learn to say no.**
- **Don't work late.**

These are all described in more detail below.

# Unclutter your life—unclutter your memory

## DRAW UP A LIFE PLAN

The important thing about a life plan is that it is not just about your work but about your whole life: work, relationships, family, friends, health, chores, and so on—each has to be fitted into the plan. There are two stages to drawing up a life plan.

### 1. Make a plan for a week

This will help you figure out:

- **What you spend most of your time doing**
- **What you don't do, but would like to do**
- **Whether you are putting enough time into your family**
- **Whether you are seeing your friends enough**
- **Whether you are keeping up with chores**

Doing this will give you a chance to look closely at your present ratio of work to home and leisure time and help you develop a plan to restore balance and also get on top of what needs to be done.

### 2. Make a plan for a month

An electronic organizer (see page 70) can be useful for this exercise, because it enables you to view a whole month at one time. Assign time to work, but actually try scheduling in blocks of time for family, friends, exercise, special interests, special projects, food shopping, paying bills, and so on. Make sure that you leave some spare time slots, since you don't want to be too regimented about life and will need to fit in things that you were not expecting, such as free time for yourself or spontaneous trips out. Avoid booking things for every night of the week, too, because you will find that if you get overtired, you will start to feel less in control and will notice that short-term memory and anything complex become quite difficult.

## USE AN ELECTRONIC ORGANIZER

One very useful device is an electronic organizer. Some organizers enable you to have the same calendar on your handheld device as well as on different computers, maybe at home and at work. When you are out and about, you can input dates on your handheld device (like a calendar), then synchronize this in the office and at home, so wherever you are you can check it. If you wish, your calendar can also be made available to a partner, to avoid double bookings.

## GET THINGS DONE

A good trick is to overestimate the time you think a job will take in order to ensure on-time delivery, even in the case of unforeseen delays, with a minimum of stress. This may even mean that you can surprise your partner or family by arriving home earlier than expected. It will impress your boss or your clients, since they will feel that they can trust you to deliver well on time and to a good standard. The most important point is that it will avoid putting you in a stressful situation, and as a result, you will be more relaxed and function much better, memory included. Here are some guidelines to help you get tasks done.

- **Break a big task down into steps.**
- **Estimate how long each step will take and make a realistic timetable.**
- **Allow enough time for unexpected delays. In the case of creative tasks, allow for inspiration time.**

## DELEGATE TASKS

Are you someone who can delegate, or do you feel any of the following:

- **It is easier to do it myself.**
- **I do it better.**
- **By the time I have explained it, I might as well do it myself.**
- **If I teach someone else, I may become less important to the company.**

It is actually a great skill to be able to delegate effectively, so, if you don't, learn to. It will free up your time. We all strive to learn, so why not delegate what you already know by teaching others? They will respect you for this. It will also leave you free to meet new challenges yourself, continuing your own learning process. It will certainly mean you are more relaxed, and this means better concentration and memory.

## MAKE LISTS

Lists are extremely rewarding. They are also a way of getting your thoughts down on paper and out of your head, thereby freeing your mind. They help you stay on top of things, and it is rewarding to check off items as they are accomplished. Develop your own list system to suit you. Here are some ideas to start you off.

- First thing in the morning, **write down everything you need to do**, big or small.
- Then **break the list down**. Put a star by the most important things that must be done that day, or list them in order of importance. Be realistic and don't hope to achieve more than you have time for.
- **Check off items** so that you can keep track of how much of the day is left and how much you still need to achieve. You will get everything done if you are organized.
- If there are lots of competing tasks that need doing, break your day down into chunks and **stick to timelines**. For example, spend the first hour of your day completing small administrative tasks. That will then free your mind to get on with each more important task in turn. By keeping on top of things, you will be able to concentrate better.
- To **get the most out of your time**, try to do your hardest jobs at those times of the day when your attention and energy levels are highest.
- Likewise, try to **schedule your routine** so that low-level tasks are done during the times of the day when you find it hard to concentrate. The trick is to pinpoint your hours of peak performance and schedule your work accordingly.

*wednesday*

Open mail. /

Pay electricity bill. /

Buy milk and eggs. /

\* Complete first draft of written report.

Check e-mail.

\* Call plumber re: tap.

Call Uncle Fred

Have lunch.

\* Act on any important e-mails or letters.

Start monthly accounts.

Check e-mail again.

Have dinner.

## LEARN TO SAY NO

We never know what to make of those (lucky) people who are "heartless" enough to say no. It is hard to do. Yet managing other people is also one of the most disruptive factors in life, and effective time-management and coping skills are dependent on you learning the skill of saying no. The good news is that it gets easier the more you do it. Contrary to popular belief, you will also be respected more. Sometimes in certain situations you can't say no, so it is important to ascertain what is important and what is not. Most things can wait.

## DON'T WORK LATE

It is almost always unnecessary to work late if you are organized. Working late makes you tired and stressed, and interferes with your free time. Of course, we all have to work late from time to time, but if you find yourself working late regularly, then it is pretty likely that you need to manage your workload better. Don't work late to impress your boss, either, because he or she may even think that you are finding it hard to keep on top of things and your attempt to make a good impression may backfire. It is much better to manage your time, work hard, stay fresh, and don't let your work encroach too much on your personal time.

We work to pay for our lives, and we should not forget that. Not only is it better for your physical health to leave work at the proper time, it is also good for your personal relationships and for your mental state. A balance is essential to both your physical and psychological well-being.

*All work and no play makes Jack a dull boy.*

# Example

It is Thursday evening. You are about to go home. You have carefully planned your week ahead, and your schedule allows you to leave by 5 P.M. so that you can go home and enjoy the summer evenings. You are feeling on top of things and relaxed, enjoying your work.

A colleague calls. She has arranged a sales demonstration on the following Monday at 3.30 P.M. She wants your input for the meeting. You are in a dilemma because you feel that it is difficult to say no.

Let's look at the two possible outcomes.

### 1. You say yes.

This means that you have to cancel the lunch meeting you had arranged with your boss to discuss your future. You have to disrupt your plans for Friday so that you can prepare your presentation. You have to drive to the meeting on Monday, which will take two and a half hours. You feel annoyed that you have been put in this spot on such short notice when it is not an urgent meeting and could have been rearranged.

You disrupt your schedule and start to feel stressed. You are in a bad mood when you get home. You are not motivated at the meeting because you don't really want to be there. You get home late on Monday, and you still have not discussed your future and now can't get another appointment with your boss for a month because he is busy, then away on vacation. Your colleague asks you next time because she knows she can rely on you to say yes.

### 2. You say no.

You think it through. You have spent time getting your schedule right for next week and everything you have booked in is important. Attending the meeting will mean that you have to cancel the lunch meeting with your boss, which you have been looking forward to for some time, as you are going to be discussing your future. The meeting is a sales meeting and it is not urgent that it be held on Monday. So you say no. You are sorry, but you are already booked that day. You comment that on the whole you need a little more warning to fit things into your busy schedule. You suggest that the meeting be rearranged and then you would be pleased to help.

Your colleague says she was not given much warning either and sounds a little disgruntled. You are pleased that you have made the right decision. It is not your problem, and just because your colleague has gotten herself into a tight spot does not mean that you should also be forced into a corner. You keep to your schedule and you remain relaxed and on top of things.

# INTEGRATING FACT WITH
# MEANING

*Human beings are special animals* with a conscious *brain and a unique way with words. From the day we are born, we learn about the world at an astonishing rate. We store large amounts of information, and it is believed that the brain has infinite capacity. This storage of information is called **memory**, and our brains are like filing systems. Memory requires effort, and we only remember what we learn. The way we learn things, however, affects how we are likely to remember them later.*

## MEANINGFUL LEARNING

Being able to recall something usually depends on how thoroughly we learned it in the first place. Practice in learning techniques can improve memory, because it means that we learn things more deeply and are more likely to store them permanently for later use. Regular review and use of information will significantly improve our retention and recall. You will learn better if you structure things, thereby giving them more meaning.

- You can make new information more meaningful by relating it to something that is already familiar or by sorting it into categories.
- The more you know about a subject, the easier it will be to understand and integrate new information.
- The more interested in something you are, the easier you will find it to learn and remember. For example, single facts are tedious, but a general overview can help make learning those facts more interesting.

## EXERCISE

Refer to the word list on page 50. Write the words down again, this time sorted into their four categories. Then try recalling the words from memory. You should find that you perform much better than the first time.

# INTEGRATING YOUR THINKING SKILLS—EXECUTIVE FUNCTIONING

There is another level above all of the individual functions described in this section, which is called **executive functioning**. Imagine memory as a big cooking pot: You need input of information, you need concentration, you need to be organized, and you need context. Throw all of these into the memory pot and then mix them all together. That is executive functioning—giving organization and order to our actions and behavior. It is like a central processing unit and involves different parts of our brain, but primarily the frontal lobes. Executive functions include planning, organizing, and controlling actions, and the ability to delay responding, to initiate behavior, to shift between activities flexibly, and to plan for the future. It is an open-ended term that is used to describe one of the hardest but most important jobs that our brains have.

What happens when your executive function is not working properly? A good example is when you have had a few drinks. You may wonder why you find yourself saying things that you might not have done when sober, behaving out of character, and so on. This is because alcohol suppresses the executive function (see also pages 124–127).

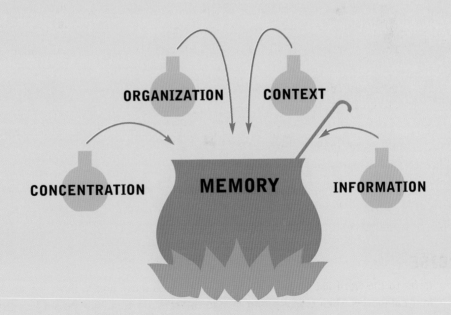

# IMPROVING
## YOUR INNER MEMORY

*Remembering* is an active process. Maximizing your memory involves paying better attention, planning, and organizing, but you can also use memory tricks or strategies. Some of these strategies come to us naturally, but it is also helpful to arm yourself with additional ones.

## Strategies

There are two main strategies:

- Inner or internal strategies help you lay down stronger memories so that you can bring information back into your mind more easily. They include effective ways of learning information and simple recall techniques such as **mnemonics**.

- Outer or external strategies are physical aids such as lists and planners. These are discussed in Step 7.

  The aim of this book is to give you an understanding of the theory of how strategies work, and when to use particular strategies.

### USING INNER STRATEGIES

This step covers inner strategies that improve active encoding and storage (including association strategies for learning, and mental rehearsal) and retrieval strategies. Of course, anything that helps encoding and storage will later help retrieval. Very importantly, too, the best way to help memory is to use strategies in combination.

## *Arm yourself with strategies.*

# ERROR-FREE LEARNING

The concept of **error-free learning** is an important one to understand. There is a myth that if you ask people to guess answers, they are more likely to remember them. In fact, they are much more likely to remember if they are guided to the right answer.

## Example

If you ask a child "Can you find your sneakers?" he may first look under the bed, then in the bathroom, and then under the stairs, where the shoes are finally found. Next time, the child's first response will probably still be to look under the bed first.

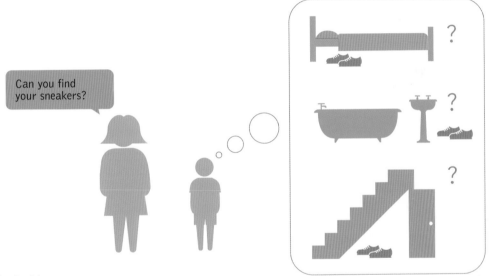

## Solution

If, instead, you were to say "Let's find your sneakers," and motion with your head or eyes toward the stairs, the child will be far more likely to produce the correct response.

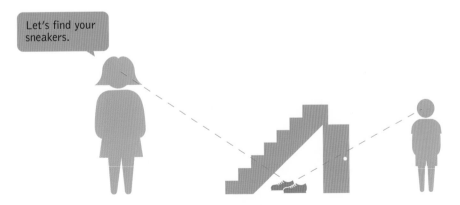

## A FEW GENERAL RULES

### Less is more

The first strategy is to ask yourself "Is this something I really need to remember?" Although your memory has a huge capacity, you do need to make a choice about what you will need to remember. Trying to remember too many new things can cause interference and overload. This will make older information more difficult to remember. To avoid this problem, a little filtering may be required.

### Can I deal with it right now?

There are often situations when you can unburden your memory system by making sure you deal with tasks as soon as they come along, meaning that you do not have to process the item any further. It is important to consider how you may save yourself the need to process information deeply so that you can attend to more important information for memory. For example, you don't need to remember everyone's telephone number, just those that you call frequently.

### Don't be afraid to ask

One good habit to develop is to discover ways of asking people for information, such as their names, that takes away the need for you to process the information and that won't make you feel embarrassed. For example, would it offend you if someone you had only met once or twice said "Now, I'm terribly sorry, but I can't remember your name?" It probably wouldn't. You might be more offended if he guessed and got your name wrong. It is probably a good idea to get him to confirm his name before you make an embarrassing mistake (and run the risk of getting it wrong next time, too).

# *You don't need to remember everyone's telephone number.*

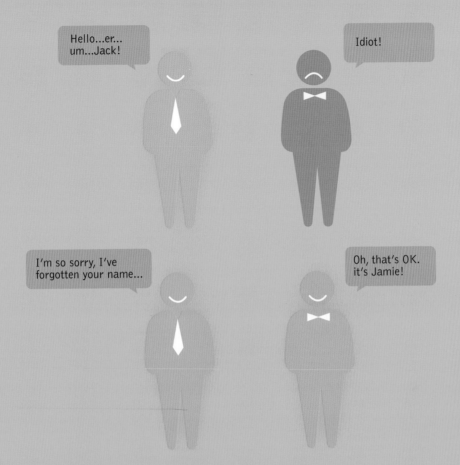

In fact, error-free learning suggests that if you were to guess at a name, then the next time you meet the same person, you could remember your wrong guess rather than the actual name. It helps your memory system to consolidate stronger correct memories by getting things confirmed rather than setting up competing ideas for situations. So, instead of guessing (even with a fifty-fifty chance), it would be better for your social graces and memory just to ask again.

# STRATEGIES
## FOR ACTIVE ENCODING AND STORAGE

### LEARNING BY ROTE

We are often in the habit of learning by repetition—for example, by reading things over and over again—and this is called **rote learning**. Research has confirmed that this method is actually not particularly effective. Imagine you are studying for a history exam. You have many different facts, dates, and names to learn about a particular topic. You have been through your notes, made a list of all the key details, and read it through many times. In the exam, you can answer the essay questions reasonably well and you cram in as many facts, dates, and names as you can remember—about 50 percent. You get a C and you are disappointed.

The problem with rote learning is that it is a shallow form of processing. To remember better, you need to learn information more deeply and encode the information in such a way that you are able to recall it effectively a long time later. To do this, you need to add meaning to your learning and use extra strategies.

### CHUNKING

Breaking down information into smaller parts can aid recall, because you are helping your memory by organizing the material. **Chunking** works well for remembering telephone numbers. You could remember the telephone number 206-411-6890 as:

| 2 | 0 | 6 | 4 | 1 | 1 | 6 | 8 | 9 | 0 |
|---|---|---|---|---|---|---|---|---|---|
| two | zero | six | four | one | one | six | eight | nine | zero |

That consists of ten chunks of information, which is too long for your working memory. If you split the number into three manageable parts, it will be easier to remember:

**206 411 6890**

This is why telephone numbers are normally broken down into several parts, separated by spaces or hyphens.

## ORGANIZATIONAL STRATEGIES

The more organized you are in your memory, the easier it is to learn and remember. Just as it is hard to find something on an untidy desk or in a messy room, it can be hard to remember something if your memory store is badly organized. Long-term memory is extremely structured, with lots of stores that have links between them. Structuring information, therefore, will help memory.

In a way, our long-term memory stores are a little like a filing cabinet or the files on a computer, with main folders divided by subject area: My accounts, My documents, My pictures, and so on. Within these quite general folders there are subfolders such as First quarter, Last week, or Vacations. As well as having particular topics, these subfolders are organized by date and time. This method of organizing information makes the information easy to retrieve when you need it.

## CONCENTRATION

This may seem obvious, but when you want to learn or remember something, make sure that you really are focusing properly on it (see also pages 64–67).

### Teaching or giving a speech

When you are presenting information to others, for example, during a speech, class, or lecture, you will need to deliver information in an organized way, combining structure with meaning and review. You will find that not only do you hold the attention of the audience better but the information is also more likely to be understood and remembered. Take them on a journey.

- Start by painting an overall picture and telling your audience what you want them to know. Present important information and summarize key points first.
- Keep to the point and reduce the amount of information you are putting across by concentrating on main points that are organized into a logical story.
- Follow this by going into detail about the different points.
- Finish by reviewing the key points once again.

# MAKING INFORMATION MEANINGFUL

Memory is a product of how well information is perceived and encoded. "Effort after meaning" gives rise to better memory. Making information meaningful therefore improves our memory by enhancing information traces that are more distinct than items that have only been remembered on a shallower level. The deeper the processing, the better you will remember.

So, if you need to remember information from a lecture, book, seminar, speech, or conversation, a key thing is to be really focused on the meaning. The point is that your memory system is making an effort to make sense of the information, so it is beneficial if you are consciously helping it do this. Asking questions can also aid our understanding.

## Socratic method

One method of making information meaningful, developed by the Greek philosopher Socrates and known as the Socratic method (and sometimes as "directed self-discovery"), involves asking some questions about what you are trying to achieve. Socratic questions tend to be ones like "What do I know already about this?" and "What might I learn from this?" In other words, you are trying to access any scripts or schemas that you may already have for a particular type of information so that you can be consciously aware of how you are adding to it.

There is a mnemonic to help people remember a script of Socratic-type questions to aid their memory: PQRST. It stands for:

- **Preview** Look over the information. What is it generally about?
- **Question** Which questions are you hoping to answer by reading or listening to the information?
- **Read** Read (or listen).
- **Summarize** What was the summary of the information?
- **Test** Have you answered all your questions?

Try **PQRST** on the next documentary TV program or newspaper article you watch or read to see if it works for you.

# To remember something, you must focus on its meaning.

## GENERATING YOUR OWN EXAMPLES

Go beyond the examples already provided on any particular topic you are trying to learn. Bring your general knowledge and experience into play by relating information and ideas to what you already know. When you can generate your own examples, you demonstrate your understanding and your memory is enhanced.

## DISCUSSING WITH OTHERS

It is extremely helpful to your memory to discuss ideas. In this way, you can verbalize what you think something means and get someone else's perspective on it. Once you have really understood and verbalized an idea, it is much easier to remember it later, and it will also become naturally integrated into the knowledge that you already have. If you do not fully understand something, or if there are gaps in your knowledge, this will become clear when you discuss it and you can then fill in those gaps.

## EXTENDING EXISTING KNOWLEDGE

Before we learn about something new, it can seem quite daunting to remember new things. Yet, as soon as we start to learn, it gets easier and easier to build up our knowledge, because it becomes more meaningful and builds up a picture. This is why we call some people experts: After developing an initial knowledge base, they have gone beyond the usual boundaries and extended their knowledge.

Imagine you have never been to a specific country, such as South Africa, but you are planning to go on vacation there. You have a specific perception, perhaps from seeing events that took place there on the news or from geography lessons at school. While you are there, you visit museums and rent a car and drive around. All the time, you are building up your memory information bank called "South Africa."

Because of your knowledge, when you now see items on the news about the country they are more meaningful, and so you take notice and listen. You understand the context, and it is easy for you to add to your knowledge and remember the information.

# ASSOCIATION
## STRATEGIES FOR LEARNING

*You can help* your memory storage system by intentionally pairing something you want to remember with something familiar—that is, you can create an **association**. Some associations are easy to make, but most things are not so obviously related and you need to be more creative to establish a link. The good news is that if you practice making associations, you will get better at it and over time will start to do it without realizing.

## USING AIDE-MÉMOIRE

These include rhymes, memorable sayings, acronyms, and other mnemonics that can be relied upon to jog your memory. You can make them up yourself to help you remember things. Be creative and clever. Be silly. The good thing is that there are already many useful aide-mémoire that most of us learned when we were young:

- **I before E, except after C**: For remembering how to spell words like "niece" and "receive"
- **Richard Of York Gave Battle In Vain**: For remembering the seven colors of the rainbow—red, orange, yellow, green, blue, indigo, and violet
- **Never Eat Shredded Wheat**: For remembering the correct order of compass points: north, east, south, west
- **Spring forward, fall back**: For remembering whether to put clocks forward or back

## *I before E, except after C.*

# VISUALIZATION

Learn to associate information with **visual images**. Difficult material can be converted into pictures and diagrams. Concrete images are more memorable than abstract ideas, and that is why pictures are more memorable. Use your mind's eye. The more silly a visualization is, the better it usually works. Visualization is a particularly useful strategy when trying to remember information about other people, because we learn about others by seeing them.

## Visualizing people's names

Remembering people's names can be greatly aided by visual images. You may notice that you remember names that are more concrete and visualizable Dakota (place) or Nat (sounds like an insect). However, most names are far more abstract (John, Peter, Joanna, Rachel), which is why we are all so bad at remembering them. Try in these instances to associate the name with a meaningful visual image.

- First, imagine how someone's name is written.
- Then try to link the name with an easily remembered visual tag, for example, Michael singing into a microphone (mic).
- For really tricky names such as Dr. Bartoleni, imagine something like a doctor leaning on a bar—Dr. Bar-to-lean-on.

| Event | Association | Visual image |
|---|---|---|
| You meet someone new. | She has the same name, Polly, as your aunt. | Imagine your new acquaintance and your aunt shaking hands. |
| You have an appointment on April 12. | Your mother's birthday is also on April 12. | Imagine being with your mother on her birthday but having to leave early for your appointment. |
| You have a new friend who likes to drink tea. | Your new friend is named Theresa. | Imagine Theresa drinking a cup of tea. |

### The image-match method

Another type of image strategy is the **image-match** method. Here, if you need to remember a particular sequence of ideas, link each one with a number and an image. For example, to recall presents you may have received from particular relatives before a party, you could visualize:

**1.** Jack in slippers
**2.** Jon drinking wine
**3.** April writing in a diary

### Visualizing by location

A useful technique is to think of a house with lots of rooms. You have several different types of information to remember, so put each type of information in a different room. When you need to remember something, mentally walk around the house, picking up the information as you go.

## Finding your way

Many people have a poor sense of direction, but this is easy to improve with practice. Try the following to get to your destination:

- Visualize a map by looking carefully at a real map and visualizing the route.
- When you are on your way, try to see the map in your mind's eye.
- If the route is intricate, add to your visual image by making an ordered list of the directions before you embark on your journey. Then you can refer to your list as you go.
- You will also have to get back afterward. When you are on the way to your destination, look for landmarks (make sure that you have paid attention to key landmarks when planning your route). This will help you get home.

# *Let landmarks guide you home.*

# MENTAL
# REHEARSAL

## ACTIVE REHEARSAL

Remember that information can only stay in your working memory for a maximum of thirty or forty seconds if it doesn't suffer interference from other information. Working memory also has a limit of about seven spaces. One way of helping to keep things available is to **rehearse** the information in your mind. Just repeat it over and over in your head. While you are rehearsing, try to add meaning to the information, since this will make it easier to remember deeply.

## EXPANDED REHEARSAL

If you need to keep information for longer, and not just between receiving information and writing it down, one very helpful strategy is to repeat the number (or list) at increasing intervals. This is known as **expanded rehearsal**. Start off with a gap of five seconds between rehearsals, then ten seconds, then twenty to forty, then sixty, and so on. This will mean that you are recalling the information within increasing time spans.

## EXERCISE

Look at the following telephone numbers, or find a number you need to remember:

(a)    **619-555-4989**
(b)    **327-555-9596**

Repeat (a) about seven times and test yourself twenty minutes later. Repeat (b) a couple of times, then again after five seconds, again after seven seconds, again after ten seconds, then twenty, thirty-five, sixty seconds, and finally five minutes.

## CLUSTERED REHEARSAL

**Clustered rehearsal** is another useful organizational memory strategy. Imagine you are asked to remember a list of items to buy while you are rushing around trying to do some last-minute Christmas shopping.

The list is: greetings cards, tangerines, a scarf, beer, wrapping paper, wine, pens, a frame, socks, tape, toothpaste, chocolate coins, brazil nuts.

To remember better, it would help to reorganize the list and repeat it as:

**Festive stationery**: greeting cards, pens, wrapping paper, tape
**Family presents**: a scarf, frame, socks
**Drinks**: beer, wine
**Holiday foods**: chocolate coins, tangerines, brazil nuts
**Extras**: toothpaste

This is effectively **highlighting** and **heading** the items and doing what is known as clustered rehearsal. The risk is that some things don't cluster well at times—such as toothpaste in this example. So it helps to add on "**Extras**: toothpaste" in your mnemonic cluster mantra.

## SUBDIVIDING CLUSTERS

Imagine now that you are able to go shopping at a more leisurely pace. You will probably have in your mind a set of needs (food, something for your baby daughter, something for work). Before you go to the mall, you may then organize this information according to which type of store you will need to visit and then imagine each of these divided into subcategories:

| Supermarket | Vegetables | Carrots, mushrooms, spinach |
| | Domestic | Detergent, trash bags |
| | Dairy | Milk, yogurt, cream |
| | Baby stuff | Cotton balls, diaper rash cream |
| **Office supplier** | Computer | Disks, printer cartridge |
| | Desk | New lamp |

## Hierarchy Trees

You will be able to remember much more of what you need if you actually put the items that you are going to get into some kind of order before you set off. A good trick is to use a hierarchy tree. Imagine the different stores as branches of a tree, categories within the stores as subbranches, and individual items as leaves on the subbranches.

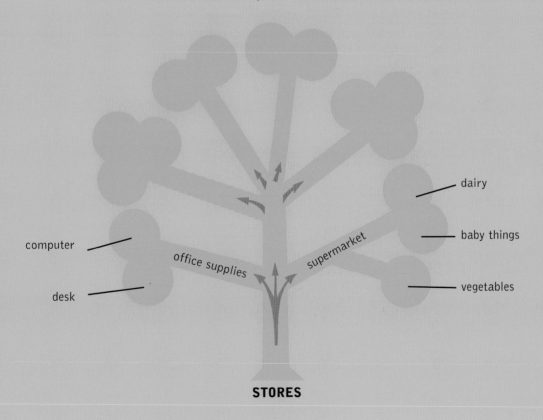

computer

desk

office supplies

supermarket

dairy

baby things

vegetables

**STORES**

# RETRIEVAL
# STRATEGIES

*If you have used* strategies for encoding and storage, your retrieval of memories should already have improved. If there is information that you want to access but you can't quite find it, however, then there are some useful strategies for that, too.

## ALPHABET SEARCHING

This means systematically going through the **alphabet** to find the first letter of the word or item you are trying to remember in order to jog your memory for it. For example, if you are trying to recall the name of an actor you recently saw in a film, start with the letter A. Think of all the actors' names you know that begin with A. Repeat with each subsequent letter until you reach the person's name. This is a little slow, but it works and is especially useful for the tip-of-the-tongue phenomenon.

## CATEGORY SEARCHING

Searching using **categories** can be an effective cue for retrieving information. For example, you have gone to the supermarket but have forgotten to take the list you had written. As you go around the aisles, think about the section you are in and think what you might have needed from that food category.

## VISUAL SEARCH OR MENTAL RETRACING

It may be possible to use a **visual search** to retrieve memories, especially for things you have misplaced. This involves **mentally retracing** your movements, activities, and thoughts in a logical sequence. For example, if you can't find your wallet, try to remember where you last paid for something. Did you put the wallet into your pocket? Check the pocket. If it isn't there, think hard about whether you have used it since or put it elsewhere.

### Example

Where did I leave my cell phone?

Before I came into this room, I checked in at reception. Before that, I was in the car. Did I leave my phone at reception? No, they would have buzzed me. Did I leave it in the car? I can't remember whether I took it to the car. OK, where was I before the car? I was at home. I remember I picked up my phone, I locked the door behind me, I had my phone in my pocket as I got into the car, and I put it in the glove compartment. Oh yes, my phone is in the glove compartment.

## CONTEXT CUING

Mentally putting yourself back in the context you were in can help you to remember better. For example, try to remember what you ate for lunch two days ago. Think back to the day in question. Where were you? Where did you have lunch? Who were you with? What did you eat? You will probably now remember.

### Summary

Retrieval strategies are helpful for processing information for particular purposes. You may need the information for only a short while or you may need it for the rest of your life. It is important to choose the strategy or strategies that are useful for you, based on your type of memory, the kind of information to be processed, and the demands being made on you.

It may take time to get into the habit of using strategies. At first it may even slow you down, but it is helpful and quite soon, it will start to pay off.

# IMPROVING
## YOUR OUTER MEMORY

*What else can we do* to help us remember better and more efficiently? There is a common misconception that if you rely on a written memory system, your memory will not improve, but clinical research actually shows the opposite is true. In fact, it is those people who write down and organize information using a structured system that show more improvement in their memory skills than those people who just try to use internal strategies (which they often forget to do). The act of writing down and thinking about information seems to exercise the memory system more than just trying to remember it.

### The eighty/twenty rule

The Italian sociologist Vilfredo Pareto (1848–1923) developed a theory that later became known as the **Pareto principle**. His observation was that many people spend eighty percent of the time they work on a project producing only about twenty percent of the results they are aiming to achieve. He considered that this was a very wasteful way of using our time and energy and identified certain "high-leverage tasks" that can be applied to our projects and work. The effect of implementing these tasks is to reverse the normal trend, so that for only twenty percent of the time spent on a project, we can achieve eighty percent of the desired results.

| High-leverage tasks | Benefits |
| --- | --- |
| Reassessing schedules | Compares where you are with where you wanted to be, and refocuses priorities |
| Setting short-term goals | Helps prioritize tasks |
| Developing relationships with key people | Has long-term benefits and helps schedules |
| Dealing with urgent and important business | Frees up time for other projects |

# Prioritizing tasks

By prioritizing your workload or other activities, you will be able to concentrate on those tasks that are crucial and thereby avoid cluttering your schedule. Divide your duties into the following four categories.

**1. Important and urgent**

Tasks that fall into this category must be done right away and are considered priorities.

**2. Important but not urgent**

These tasks are still very important, but because they are not urgent, they can be completed at an appropriate time in the future.

**3. Urgent but not important**

These are the main cause of disruption for you, because they are tasks that are often urgent for others but not important for you. Your options are to say no, to find someone else to do the task, or to negotiate an alternative deadline.

**4. Not urgent and not important**

These tasks can be safely ignored (until they move up into one of the other categories).

# Other methods

## USING STRATEGIES

Strategies that will help you improve your outer memory include the following:

- **Planning**
- **Setting goals**
- **Building relationships**
- **Setting up effective systems and procedures**
- **Developing key skills**

## HELPING YOUR EPISODIC MEMORY

It is easy to help yourself to remember when and where you did things simply by using a calendar or an electronic organizer. As part of your plan, you will have recorded when and where you have things happening in your life. You may even want to keep a planner if you want to remember what you do in detail.

## HELPING YOUR SEMANTIC MEMORY

Improving your memory for facts and information is aided by an organized system for recording names, dates, phone numbers, addresses, and conversations. Use a personal tape recorder to record lectures and meetings, and to make your own comments. Write up notes and tag them with associations to help you remember them. Organize your filing system so that you can refer back when you need to.

*Organizing your filing system will organize your memory.*

# MANAGING
## DAILY AFFAIRS

*Some of the simplest* things to remember can be the most annoying when forgotten: not being able to find your keys, leaving your cell phone somewhere, forgetting to pay a bill, not remembering what time an appointment was. These are everyday problems that we all have at times, but they are the easiest to solve—all you need to do is become more organized and use a few external aids.

### Improving your organization

- **Don't lose everyday objects**
  Get into the habit of always putting things in the same place. For example, for your keys, try putting a row of hooks up by the door and always put your keys there.

- **File important information**
  Keep separate files for bank statements, bills, and so on. This system will help you remember what you have done and what you need to do.

- **Make lists**
  List all the things that you need to do, remembering to prioritize. Then cross the items off as you finish them.

- **Decide what you need for the next day**
  Each evening, think through what you will need for the next day, and pack your bag or briefcase the night before. This will prevent a last-minute rush and forgetting important items that you will need for the day. Keep a list by the door and check that you have everything before you leave for the day.

### Using external aids
- When traveling, write down the directions in advance and take them with you.
- Keep a notepad by the telephone to record messages.
- Use a wall calendar to mark appointments and other important information.
- Keep a calendar to track appointments and meetings.

# MANAGING
# DISTRACTIONS

*When we complain* that we can't concentrate, we usually mean that we can't keep our attention on what we are trying to do because of various distractions, both external and internal. Learning to manage distractions will help you start to focus your attention in the desired direction.

## EXTERNAL DISTRACTIONS

There is a huge number of external distractions that can seriously affect your concentration and memory, whether you are at home or in an office environment. These include televisions, radios, telephones, lighting levels, temperature, people's voices, traffic noise, and so on. You may think that there is nothing you can do to reduce these distractions, but some of them are definitely within your control:

- Turn off the television or radio. Reward yourself with your favorite programs at lunchtime or in the evening.
- Turn off your cell phone. You can check it for messages at lunchtime or in the afternoon.
- Turn off your e-mail. E-mail may be one of the worst external distractions of modern times. Again, just check at sensible intervals throughout the day.

## *Turn off the television and turn on your attention.*

## Controlling your environment

Other things may also be within your control, especially if you work from home:

- Adjust the room temperature and lighting levels until you feel perfectly comfortable.
- Arrange your workstation or desk so that you are less likely to be bothered by noise such as traffic or phones ringing—maybe raise a partition or face away from an open window.

# INTERNAL DISTRACTIONS

You may be thinking of other things—what you are going to have for lunch, that bill that arrived this morning in the mail, what you are doing tonight, what the person you are talking to is wearing, and so on. These are all distracting thoughts that will interfere with your ability to get on with things and to take in information. For example, how often do any of the following apply to you?

- You read a paragraph and at the end you can't actually remember what it was about.
- You have a conversation with someone and then forget what the point of it was.
- You ask for directions, but forget most of what you are told.
- You don't remember the name of someone you are introduced to in a meeting.
- You are unable to concentrate when taking exams or listening to talks or lectures.

## Coping with internal distractions

There are many ways in which we can learn to cope with internal distractions, enabling us to concentrate and thus remember better.

### 1. Use external aids.

These can free your mind of distractions. Keep a notepad handy and jot down all the things you need to do today. As new things come up, add to the list so that you don't worry about remembering (worrying keeps you from concentrating and processing properly). As you do each item, cross it off your list. This will make you feel that you are getting somewhere, and so you will relax and concentrate better.

### 2. Listen properly.

If you are in a class or lecture, your natural tendency may be to try to write everything down. A much better way, however, is to sit back, relax, and listen to what the person is saying, thereby building up a picture of the subject matter. It is always helpful if you get the lecture notes, so you are free to actually listen. What most people don't realize is that most subject matter is already written in detail in textbooks, so these can be referred to later on. The important thing is to listen in the first place.

3. **Use a timetable that includes regular breaks.**

   For tasks such as studying for an exam or working on a project, draw up a timetable that ensures you start and finish work at regular times each day and that you take regular breaks at preplanned times. You should also take evenings and weekends off. If you have concentrated properly on the timetable, you should be able to do what you need to without working all day and night—this will only make you tired and irritable, and far less able to concentrate.

4. **Clear your mind.**

   If you have a significant task to achieve, try to complete all other tasks the day before you begin or put aside the first hour of the day to do this, so that you can clear your mind of internal distractions. Say no to any other work or distractions. (See also Step 9 about how to improve your concentration and memory through a healthier lifestyle—this is particularly important when you are trying to accomplish an important task.)

5. **Have a positive attitude.**

   If you view a task as boring, it will be increasingly difficult to concentrate on it. However, most things are not as boring as you may think, and if you take a different, more positive approach and try to see the interesting side or feel pleased that you are contributing to your knowledge, it will seem much easier.

*Things are not as boring as you may think.*

# TIPS FOR BEING BETTER
# ORGANIZED

## PLAN THE NEXT WEEK

On a Friday afternoon, think about the following week. Make a list of things that you need to complete at work, at home, or in your studies. Prioritize the items and try to be realistic about what you can do. Look at what you are planning to do in context of time and other work, and decide if you are planning to make the most of your time. Writing a list like this at the end of the week clears your mind for the weekend, which means you can relax, knowing that you are in control. When Monday morning comes, you know you will be able to finish what you need to during the following week and will not forget important items.

## PLAN THE NEXT DAY

You can extend this system by having a modified list for each day. Try to check off all items before the end of the day and then you will be able to relax in the evening, sleep better, and be fresh for another day.

| mon | tues | wed | thur | fri | sat | sun |
|---|---|---|---|---|---|---|
|  |  | 1 planning meeting 3.30 pm | 2 painting class | 3 | 4 visit parents | 5 |
| 6 | 7 | 8 | 9 painting class | 10 | 11 | 12 Mom's birthday |
| 13 | 14 School term starts | 15 | 16 painting class | 17 Dentist 2 pm | 18 | 19 tennis 2 pm |
| 20 pay phone bill | 21 | 22 Finish Report | 23 painting class | 24 | 25 day trip | 26 |
| 27 | 28 phone accountant | 29 | 30 painting class |  |  |  |

## USE A CALENDAR

Hang a big calendar on the wall at home. Itemize all your different tasks, appointments, classes, and so on, and write items in as they are booked. Do this in advance (you may prefer to use either a weekly or a monthly calendar), and make sure you understand exactly what you are doing and when. You can always refer to it if you forget anything.

# Get ready for Monday morning.

## USE A NOTEBOOK

If you wake up in the morning with many things on your mind, try writing down your thoughts and tasks in a notebook. It is best to use a colorful notebook that you can find easily, that will not fall apart, and that has numbered pages. Write the date in for each entry, since this can also be a useful reference when you forget something.

## PAY YOUR BILLS

Bills often come in and are overlooked for weeks or get lost in a pile of paperwork until a final reminder arrives. Keep a basket or box in a prominent place (the kitchen, for example) and put all your unpaid bills in there so that they are constantly in view. Pay each bill as soon as you can and write the date and method of payment on it so that you have a record of when and how you paid it. Then file all paid bills away according to type (gas, electricity, water, and so on).

## ORGANIZE YOUR RECORDS

If you are self-employed, for example, it is useful to have a similar system for receipts and other paperwork—there is nothing more tedious than having to hunt around for a year's worth of receipts, bank statements, invoices, and so on. Start a file for the year and update it every few months. Also consider using a spreadsheet on a computer to keep track of your budget month by month; this will save time and help you monitor your financial position.

# QUICK REFERENCE GUIDE TO COMMON SITUATIONS

*There are certain situations* that are common to many people: being in the office, preparing for exams, working from home, organizing everyday affairs, dealing with everyday memory problems, and dealing with memory changes as you get older. In Step 8, a number of specific common scenarios are described, with advice about how to deal with them.

## Coping at work

At work, by far the biggest obstacle to completing projects is the sheer number of tasks most of us face each day. Progress in a particular task will be halted by dealing with emergencies in other jobs, and this can often lead to stress. If you focus your energies on achieving your goals and managing distractions at work, you will be able to function much more efficiently in all aspects of your life, thereby reducing the amount of stress that may be affecting your memory, as well as your general well-being.

### ACHIEVING YOUR GOALS

The first aim should be to try to achieve all of the goals you set yourself for each day or week. Case studies A and B show two different scenarios.

*Learn how to put out office fires.*

## Case study A

Peter is always busy. He returns home from work each evening thinking he has achieved very little. He is tired and usually frustrated by the end of the day because he finds himself drawn in to other people's demands and requests. This gets in the way of success in achieving the goals and tasks he sets for himself for the day.

### The problem

Peter has not prioritized his day-to-day work and is constantly caught up in reactive activities that are usually driven by the priorities of others.

### The solution

This pattern may sound familiar. There are two things Peter can do to manage his priorities more effectively and stay focused on his important tasks and goals:

1. **Prioritize** (see page 93). By prioritizing his workload, Peter will be able to concentrate on crucial tasks and thereby avoid cluttering his schedule with irrelevant duties.

2. **Apply the eighty/twenty rule** (see page 92). If Peter spends a period of time implementing strategies (planning, setting goals, building relationships, setting up effective systems and procedures, developing key skills) for each task, he will soon find they progress more smoothly and he will free up some time for managing on-the-spot problems.

## Case study B

Val is a very good planner. She spends Sunday evenings with her husband and two teenage children planning the week ahead—establishing tasks for the family and identifying and removing overlaps in their busy schedules. She spends the time she saves with her family and in converting an unused bedroom into a study. Val has identified planning the family week as one of her high-leverage tasks (see page 92), which, for just a small amount of effort, enables her and the members of her family to spend more time together and also allows her time to complete a project.

**Val's success** lies in the fact that she has identified planning the family week as a high-leverage task. She and her family save valuable time during the week by being organized and planning ahead, which only takes a minimal amount of time on a Sunday evening.

## MANAGING OFFICE DISTRACTIONS

Many people now work in open-plan offices. While this setup can have its advantages, learning to manage such an environment can be quite a skill in itself. In addition, there are e-mails, faxes, and phone calls to respond to, and sometimes it seems as though you can never get a moment to actually do your work. So how can you manage your environment to optimize your performance and prevent yourself from being distracted? Look at case study C.

*Arrange your workstation to beat open-plan distractions.*

## Case study C

Jenny is a diligent manager in an insurance company. She sits within a "subspace" of four people. She has a coworker sitting directly opposite her. Her desk is next to the main hallway.

### The problem

Jenny finds that it is very difficult to get going on her work for any length of time because people walking down the hall often stop and chat. Her immediate work colleagues don't think twice about asking her questions, which break her concentration. She can also hear other people talking on the telephone over the partition.

### The solution

There are various things you can do to improve a situation such as the one Jenny finds herself in.

- Alter your workstation so that you are facing away from the hallway and anyone walking past—they will be less likely to distract you from behind. This will also mean that you are not staring directly at your colleague sitting opposite.

- Schedule in regular meeting times for your immediate colleagues to ask questions.

- If possible, raise the partition so that you can't see or hear people on the other side.

- Turn off your e-mail. Check it a few times a day.

- Make your phone calls in specific time slots and encourage your immediate colleagues to do the same.

- When trying to get something done, let your calls go to voice mail and then make return calls in blocks.

# EVERYDAY
## MEMORY PROBLEMS

*This area of difficulty* includes forgetting names and numbers, forgetting where you put things, not being able to recall a date or other historical fact, forgetting what you went into a room for, and so on. The good news is that although just about everyone suffers the same problems, they are actually relatively easy to overcome with a little practice.

## REMEMBERING NAMES

Many people think they have a bad memory because they cannot remember names. If you are one of them, rest assured you are not alone. The first point about names is that they are actually very abstract and therefore hard to "tag." The reason we remember some names better than others is usually for a reason. For example, it is easier to remember names like Dakota, Nat, and Daisy than ones like Gary, Peter, or John, partly because they are more unusual but also because they are more "imagable"—that is, you can associate them with a place, an insect, and a flower. So you need to make associations. Try the following when you are introduced to someone:

- First, listen carefully to his name.
- Say his name back to him: "Nice to meet you, John."
- Use his name once again: "So, John, what do you do?" This helps to cement his name into your memory.
- Visualize his name in your mind's eye, that is, the individual letters that make up the name—J O H N.
- Associate his name with something, if you can. For example, John is from Ohio, wears glasses, has a prominent brow, and has brown hair. This will be particularly useful when you see him again and need to jog your memory for his name.
- It is also helpful to envisage the person in a silly scenario—John sitting on the top of a mountain, looking for his glasses, while furrowing his brow.

# How to remember John...

This is John...

Nice to meet you, JOHN

Glasses, pinstripe suit, J-O-H-N

## REMEMBERING NUMBERS AND DATES

This is another everyday difficulty. For dates, keep a calendar and always review a week ahead. For important numbers, try the following techniques:

- Break them down into chunks.
- Visualize the numbers written down.
- See the spatial pattern that they make on the keypad (on both telephone and ATM).
- Try using the expanded rehearsal technique described on page 87.

You don't need to remember every number, however, so for other numbers use other methods:

- Write them down.
- Store them in your cell phone, if you have one.

## NOT LOSING EVERYDAY ITEMS

Be organized and try to form the habit of always putting things back in the same place. If you have lost something and need to find it quickly:

- Think back to where you last had the item.
- Try to visualize what you did with it.
- Look in the places you usually leave it.

## REMEMBERING WHAT YOU WENT INTO A ROOM FOR

Work through these steps until you remember:

- Concentrate and try not to be distracted by other thoughts.
- Think back to where you came from and mentally retrace your steps.
- Return to the place you started from. This puts you in the original context and prompts your memory.

## THE TIP-OF-THE-TONGUE PHENOMENON

We are all familiar with this one—something such as the name of a famous person, a character in a book, or a particular place is just on the tip of your tongue, but you can't quite recall it. Try these steps to trigger recall:

- Go through the alphabet and think of words or names beginning with each letter.
- Think of a context or related item as a prompt.
- Relax—stress will keep you from remembering.
- Visualize what the person or item looks like and build up a mental picture.

## FINDING YOUR WAY AROUND

Before you leave for somewhere you have not been before, take time to:

- Plan a route using a map.
- Visualize the route in your head to create a mental picture so you can get to your destination by memory (rather than having to stop and check).
- Circle the place you are going to on the map, so that if you need to refer to the map you can find it quickly.
- Make a list (using bullet points and large writing) of the directions to refer to during the journey.

When you are asking for directions to somewhere:

- Listen carefully to what the person you have asked is saying. Try to focus on what he is saying (not what he is wearing, for example).
- Visualize what he is saying.
- Summarize the instructions back to him—"So I should go left, right, right again, then left."
- Before you proceed, take a moment to run through the instructions, then repeat them to yourself as you go on your way.
- If the other person is speaking too fast or not clearly enough, slow him down by repeating each step as he says it.

# *What did I come in here for?*

# STUDYING FOR EXAMS

*Exams can strike fear* into anyone. Just when we need it most, our memory fails us and we fail the exam, even though we were perfectly capable of passing it. The way we study, however, can have a significant effect on our eventual performance inside the exam room.

### Case study D

Sarah never does very well in her exams. She puts off studying until two weeks before the exam because she doesn't think she will be able to remember as well if she tries to study earlier. Then she panics as she starts to study and realizes just how much she has to learn. "Just how am I going to get all this information in?" However much she reads through her

notes, they just don't seem to sink in. She works all hours of the day and night and drinks lots of coffee to try to help her stay alert. She feels guilty if she takes breaks. Before she goes into the exam, she gets very stressed because she just doesn't feel prepared, and when she sits down to begin, her mind goes blank. She doesn't seem to remember anything. She decides she just isn't smart enough.

### Case study E

David does very well on his exams. He plans a studying timetable for weeks ahead, allowing weekends and evenings off. He makes sure he exercises each day and eats properly. He arranges study sessions with fellow students to discuss specific topics. He summarizes his notes and visualizes the order of his notes on one side of a piece of paper.

When he arrives at the exam, he is rested because he has had a good night's sleep. He feels prepared and so is relaxed and can concentrate. He thoroughly understands his subject, so is able to adapt his knowledge to the way the questions are phrased. He feels confident he will do well.

# HOW TO STUDY EFFECTIVELY

Case studies D and E illustrate two different ways of approaching the task of studying for an exam.

## Summary

John's studying is much more effective than Sarah's. In order to follow his example, try out the following plan.

- Make sure you go to all the classes or lectures, listen carefully, think the topic through, and ask questions. Questioning can help to clarify points that you have not fully understood, and a better understanding will help you to process information better.
- When you start studying, develop a timetable and stick to it. Allow enough time for relaxation and rewards (lunch, a cookie in the afternoon, and so on).
- Start by reading through notes of a particular topic and summarize the main points.
- Do some extra reading to make the notes more memorable, meaningful, and interesting. Try to see the connection between different topics so that you build up a more meaningful picture.
- Lie down, close your eyes, and try to understand the material. It can help to discuss the topic with someone from the same class. Unless you have really understood something, it is hard to reproduce it in an exam.
- For formulas, quotes, and similar material, try to create an aide-mémoire (see page 84) to make them more memorable and give you a memory "tag."
- Just before the exam, visualize the serial order of the main points as you have written them down. In the exam, "see" the list in your mind's eye.
- Physical health is important, so eat properly and get enough sleep.

# *Beat the fear through work, rest, and rewards.*

# GETTING
# OLDER

*Memory lapses happen* more often as we get older because just as with our bodies, our brains start to change. Common memory problems may become more frequent. Changes in vision and reduced hearing can also affect memory performance. The speed at which we can process information changes, too, and we become less "flexible."

*As we age, the ability to take in new information and to recall things is particularly affected. There are lots of differences between individuals, but normal aging usually only causes mild or occasional difficulties. However, such memory changes can provoke feelings of loss, anxiety, and frustration. Understanding such feelings can be an enormous help.*

## ASSESSING YOUR GENERAL HEALTH

If you feel you are losing your memory and are worried that this might be due to some form of illness, the following formal and informal checks should help to reassure you.

- Discuss your changing memory with friends. You will probably find that they worry, too.
- Don't panic when you read an article on Alzheimer's disease in the paper—the memory changes associated with disease are very different from those found in aging.
- Arrange an appointment with an optician for an eye test, and wear glasses if you need them.
- Have a hearing test and don't be ashamed to wear a hearing aid—it will improve your quality of life markedly, and other people around you will thank you for it.
- In some areas, there are specialty screening clinics where you don't even need a referral from your doctor. About 90 percent of people worry unnecessarily, but getting tested can be a huge relief and put your mind at ease.
- If you are still worried, arrange to see your doctor for a checkup.

## Using strategies

Try the following strategies to aid your memory:

- Keep a notepad by the phone to record calls and messages.
- Put essential information on your refrigerator.
- Don't be afraid of writing things down to help you to remember.
- Put items such as keys and glasses in a specific place and keep them only in this place.
- Attach keys or glasses to a neck cord.
- Use a wall calendar to mark appointments and other important information, then get into the habit of looking at this every day.
- Keep a planner both for future appointments and to refer back to what you have done in the past.
- Make lists of things to do and check each one off when done.
- Use a personal voice recorder to speak into when you think of things you will need to do later. You can then replay the messages to remind yourself.
- When traveling, write down the directions in advance and take them with you.
- If you regularly take medication, buy a pill box marked with the days of the week on it. Prepare the pills for the week in advance on a particular day.

If you start to develop such habits and routines it will help you to remember and feel organized, and will make you feel less anxious. If you do get stressed, try to carry out simple relaxation and breathing exercises. Examples of these are listening to relaxing music, taking a warm bath with scented oils, gardening, and taking walks. Finally, it is very important to:

- Keep physically healthy—eat sensibly and exercise regularly.
- Keep mentally active (do puzzles and games, attend discussion groups, and so on).

# *Don't panic—aging has only a minor effect on memory.*

# CHANGING
## YOUR LIFESTYLE

*Perfectly healthy lifestyles* are rare in the real world. We all have our vices and are regularly tempted by things that are not necessarily good for us. For example, many of us will occasionally drink too much alcohol or eat too many high-fat or sugary foods. The bad news is that the state of our physical health tends to go hand in hand with our mental health, and what we eat and how we live our lives also affects our memory function.

## Being realistic

We can't get away from the fact that improved health improves overall well-being, as well as having secondary effects on memory and concentration—that is, the ability to lay down new memories and learn. If, at the very least, we become more aware of the impact of different lifestyle factors, we can then understand why we may experience problems and begin to do something about it. The best any of us can do is strive for a healthier lifestyle and feel pleased with ourselves when we succeed.

## Exercising mind and body

This step reviews a number of lifestyle factors and how they impact on our memory, including exercise, diet, stress, and sleep. A greater understanding of these areas will help you on the path to a better memory and may help to preserve it for longer. Both our bodies and our minds benefit from regular stimulation; like a machine, if neglected, they will function less well and eventually break down. You need to find a level of exercise, both physical and mental, that you are comfortable with and that you are likely to stick to.

## MENTAL EXERCISE

There is evidence that mental exercise is essential for keeping the brain active and healthy. It helps to release certain chemicals that are important to immune system function, thereby protecting the brain from disease and deterioration. Intellectual challenges may even stimulate the growth of new brain cells.

Exercising your brain is to be recommended at all stages of life but is especially important when we become older. If your daily work does not provide you with mental stimulation, try:

- Doing crosswords
- Doing puzzles
- Playing chess
- Playing card games, such as bridge
- Reading books, journals, or magazines
- Joining a discussion group
- Attending an evening class

Some of these activities are also very sociable, so they may also help you to avoid succumbing to problems such as loneliness, stress, or depression.

# *Take your mind to the gym daily.*

## PHYSICAL EXERCISE

Exercise helps to maintain a healthy blood-sugar level. It also releases positive chemicals in the brain, which can help stimulate memory function. Exercise also helps us to cope with stress and to stay healthy, all of which lead to better concentration and memory. If you are the type of person who loves to work out at the gym or swim for thirty or forty minutes several times a week, there is no problem. If not, however, there are plenty of other ways to make sure you are getting regular physical exercise:

• For short journeys, walk rather than drive.
• Take the stairs instead of the elevator or escalator.
• Join a fitness, dance, or yoga class.
• If you work in an office, go out for a walk at lunchtime rather than staying at your desk.
• Go jogging or play tennis with friends on a regular basis.

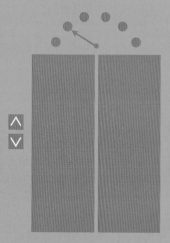

Taking the stairs instead of the elevator can improve your health—and your memory.

# GETTING A GOOD NIGHT'S SLEEP

*There is a lot of evidence* to show that sleep is important for mental and psychological well-being. This does not mean that a few bad nights' sleep will be a problem, but it does mean that trying to make sure that you have a reasonable sleep pattern will be a good thing for your memory. Ironically, too much sleep has the same effect as too little sleep. Therefore you will need to find the correct balance.

## EFFECTS OF LACK OF SLEEP

You may find it relatively easy to function for short periods of time on little sleep, but you will also find that your memory recall becomes poor and that you find it difficult to take things in. Sleepiness in the waking state impairs memory formation and retrieval. Sleep-loss studies, sedative-drug studies, and studies of patients with disorders of excessive sleepiness have all found memory impairment.

Many of these studies show that the degree of memory impairment is consistent with the degree of waking sleepiness. Many otherwise healthy people continually deprive themselves of adequate sleep, with consequences that include fatigue, poor decision-making, and increased risk of accidents. Lack of sleep may also affect the absorption of glucose, which we know is involved in good memory (see page 122). Chronic sleep loss may not only hasten the onset but also increase the severity of age-related ailments such as diabetes, hypertension, obesity, and memory loss.

Further studies have shown that making sure children get a good night's sleep leads to better performance and better test results. There are also studies to show that people learn procedural skills (physical routines) better if they have a good sleep routine. You will remember more and perform far better on that exam or at that big meeting if you have slept properly rather than spent all night preparing.

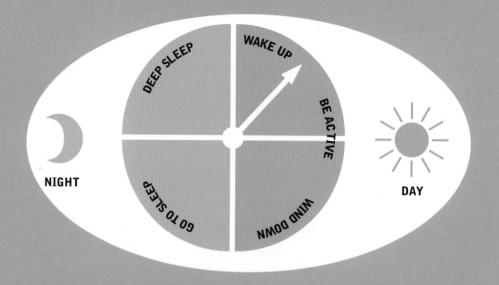

## YOUR BODY CLOCK

Having a good sleep pattern allows us to live more sympathetically with our natural body rhythms. Our biological clock consists of built-in rhythms within our body that respond to natural cycles such as light and dark. That is why we tend to find it easier to get up in the light summer mornings and feel more tired when it grows dark early on winter evenings. Although it is difficult to achieve, since we all have varied and often not routine lifestyles, it is easier to function effectively when we follow a regular pattern of sleeping and rising at the same time each day.

### The link between dreams and memory

There are five stages of sleep, and the deepest (and most active) of these is **Rapid Eye Movement** (**REM**) sleep, so called because the eyes flicker back and forth. In REM, the brain and body both become active, increasing heart rate and blood pressure.

REM sleep is most often associated with dreaming, and it is thought that dreaming helps consolidate memories. In REM sleep, our minds are working out issues and anxieties in our waking life, as well as creating space for imagination, free association, and playfulness, all of which foster creativity and analytical thinking.

## OVERCOMING JET LAG

Jet lag is a common cause of memory difficulties. It happens when a traveler in a plane passes over a number of time zones and disrupts the normal circadian rhythms that help humans wake up in the morning and go to sleep at night. It can make you feel exhausted and disoriented, and disrupts your sleep pattern. Some recent evidence even suggests that individuals who fly regularly and repeatedly suffer from jet lag could be permanently affecting their brain function. Women, in general, suffer worse jet lag than men. If you have to fly, try the following:

- Eat only light meals and drink only water (but lots of it).
- Do exercises and relax as much as you can.
- Try to sleep for a reasonable period (don't watch films all night).
- Don't take artificial sleep aids—sleeping pills adversely affect memory and complex processing in the brain.

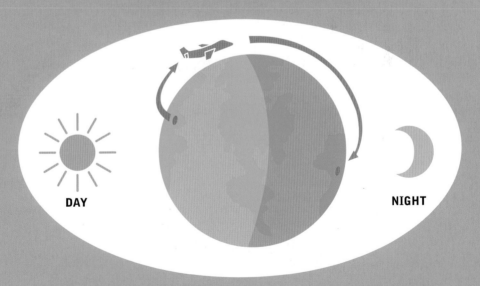

**DAY**

**NIGHT**

## *Jet lag confuses your body clock.*

# TEN TIPS FOR A GOOD NIGHT'S SLEEP

If you have trouble sleeping, try following these ten simple rules, and you may find there is a big improvement in your sleeping patterns. Remember, however, that these are only tips—we all have our own ways that suit us best.

**1.** Get into a regular routine. Go to bed and get up at roughly the same time each day. Get a sense of what your best level of sleep is—maybe six, eight, or ten hours. We are all different.

**2.** If you want to establish a good routine, don't be tempted to sleep in to catch up on sleep. Try to start by getting up at the same time and going to bed when you are tired. You should find yourself drifting into sleepiness earlier in the evening. After a few days, you will start to get tired at a regular time.

**3.** Avoid drinks with caffeine in them in the evenings. Most people know that coffee has a lot of caffeine in it, but people are not usually so aware that tea and soft drinks also contain caffeine.

**4.** Don't drink excessive amounts of alcohol (see pages 124–127). Alcohol is a depressant and can therefore put you into a state of low mental arousal. It also disrupts sleep cycles.

**5.** Plan your day so that you are tackling more taxing and engaging tasks later in the morning and midafternoon, then do relaxing activities in the evening.

**6.** Be aware that watching television or reading can be overstimulating, and may cause you to toss and turn.

**7.** If you have things running through your mind, write them down before you go to bed. If they become nagging thoughts, write them down on a pad next to your bed.

**8.** Avoid sleeping during the day.

**9.** If you are not asleep after fifteen to thirty minutes, get out of bed and do something relaxing until you feel sleepy. The point is that you don't want your body to implicitly learn that bed is somewhere where you mull things over restlessly and feel agitated.

**10.** The bedroom is not a kitchen or living room. Don't eat, watch television, or read in it. It's a bedroom—let your body associate it with things that are meant for the bedroom.

## THE BENEFITS

Sleep abnormalities tend to disappear when a normal sleep pattern is resumed. So, if you are a busy person who needs to work late occasionally, don't turn this into a habit. Learn to prioritize better so that you can get a full night's sleep more often. You will feel far better and perform at your optimum level, which in the long run will be much more beneficial for you, as well as for those around you.

# How much sleep do *you* need to function properly?

# What affects *your* sleep patterns?

# IMPROVING YOUR DIET

*Medical professionals* have known for years that a healthy diet and a moderate amount of exercise are the key to increasing energy and preventing certain types of disease. Improving one's diet is not as difficult as people think, even in our busy, stressful lives. It is becoming much easier to buy varied, tasty, nutritious foods.

## THE EFFECTS OF DIET

It is now well established that a diet high in saturated fat and highly processed foods is detrimental to brain function and may even contribute to the onset of dementia later in life.

## NATURAL GLUCOSE

To function properly, the brain needs energy in the form of natural glucose (found mainly in fruit and vegetables). When glucose metabolism is impeded by saturated fatty acids, it is like starving the brain of energy.

## THE MEDITERRANEAN DIET

The benefits of the typical Mediterranean diet, which includes plenty of extra-virgin olive oil, are now well established. It appears that high monounsaturated fatty acid intakes, mostly present in vegetable oils and particularly in extra-virgin olive oil, may help maintain the structure of brain cell membranes. Such diets may also stave off age-related memory loss in healthy, elderly people.

## ESSENTIAL NUTRIENTS

The nutrients in the food we eat are needed to keep the brain in good working order. Good-quality ingredients provide this raw material to build and fuel brain power.

- **Water** is essential to keep the body cleansed and to carry away waste products, and is good for concentration and alertness.
- **Proteins** provide the "structural building materials" for the brain and are essential for improving mental functions, as well as lifting spirits. They are found in meat, fish, milk, eggs, cheese, beans, and grains.
- **Carbohydrates** provide the brain with energy and keep glucose levels stable. They are found in grains, fruits, and vegetables.
- **Essential fatty acids** are needed to improve vision and to aid learning and memory. They are found in oily fish (such as salmon, mackerel, and sardines), nuts, and seeds.
- **B-complex vitamins** are especially important to the brain and have key roles in producing energy. They are found in liver, cabbage, cauliflower, caviar, eggs, lentils, and soy products.
- **Vitamins A, C, and E** are antioxidants and promote and preserve memory (particularly in the elderly). They are found in fruits and vegetables.

## Memory-booster foods

A diet rich in fruits and vegetables will help protect the brain and preserve memory. These will also help to boost levels of dopamine—an essential chemical in our brain associated with memory and mood. This is found in berries, carrots, sweet potatoes, watercress, peas, oily fish, and brewer's yeast. Other foods that aid with brain function include red peppers, onions, broccoli, beets, tomatoes, beans, nuts, seeds, molasses, lean meats, and soy products.

# REDUCING
# YOUR ALCOHOL INTAKE

*Alcohol affects* your memory. Even a small, regular amount can make you less sharp. Yet it is a fact of life that most people like a drink or two, and most of us probably drink too much. Alcohol is associated with relaxation and can enhance social situations. As well as this, many of us may drink alcohol as a reaction to a stressful day. When relaxing in the evening, over a meal, or watching television, once you have opened a bottle of wine it is all too easy to drink more than just a glass or two.

*Remember that alcohol is a drug. It is not difficult to fall into the habit of regularly drinking just a little too much, and then it can start to have a negative, cumulative effect on your optimal memory performance. This section provides guidelines on how to reduce your overall consumption to established safe or low-risk levels, and to keep it there.*

## HOW DOES ALCOHOL AFFECT MEMORY?

Alcohol has a powerful impact on both learning and memory. It affects the release of chemicals in the brain (called glutamate and GABA), which in turn interferes with the brain's ability to form new memories, particularly memories for facts, such as names or phone numbers, and events, such as what you did last night. Even low doses of alcohol disrupt your ability to form memories for small pieces of information. Alcohol also reduces your ability to retrieve previously formed memories and can cause the tip-of-the-tongue phenomenon.

### Binge drinking

Drinking far too much at one time, known as **binge drinking**, causes complete memory loss, and regularly doing this is extremely bad for the memory. People who drink excessively for a long period can even develop Korsakoff's syndrome—a form of dementia in which the brain loses its ability to recover. This causes profound and permanent memory loss.

# GENDER DIFFERENCES

Women may suffer the effects of alcohol more strongly than men. This is because men have a higher total body water content, and so alcohol is diluted and more efficiently eliminated from their bodies. Women tend to store alcohol at higher concentrations and for longer in their bodies, and as a result are more susceptible to impaired memory and concentration. There may also be an interaction between the menstrual cycle and female sex hormones, meaning that alcohol affects a woman in different ways at different times of the month.

## Safer alcohol limits

We are all different—size, weight, sex, age, and tolerance levels are individual, and you will need to learn about your own acceptable intake. The recommended amounts are given below (a standard drink, or unit, denotes: one bottle of beer, one single measure of liquor, one small glass of wine, or one measure of aperitif).

- Men: No more than fifteen units per week, but preferably no more than two per day, with two alcohol-free days per week.
- Women: No more than ten units per week, but preferably no more than one or two drinks per day, with two alcohol-free days per week.
- Pregnant women: No alcohol.
- If you have a physical alcohol dependence: No alcohol.
- If you suffer from physical problems that are made worse by drinking: No alcohol.
- If you are driving, riding a bike, operating machinery, or exercising: No alcohol.

bottle of beer
**= 1 UNIT**

glass of wine
**= 1 UNIT**

measure of liquor
**= 1 UNIT**

measure of aperitif
**= 1 UNIT**

## The dreaded hangover

Hangovers make us feel terrible for several reasons:

- **Buildup of toxins**

  An overdose of alcohol introduces toxins into your body faster than the body can flush them out. This results in various unpleasant effects, such as a severe headache. The toxins can also irritate your stomach, causing sickness.

- **Dehydration**

  Drinking alcohol causes you to lose more fluid than you take in, causing headaches and other symptoms, such as dizziness.

- **Lack of proper sleep**

  Your sleep pattern changes when you have drunk a large amount of alcohol, preventing certain deep stages of sleep and dreaming, so lack of quality sleep contributes to the general grumpiness and fatigue you feel as part of a hangover.

## AGE

As we get older, our bodies become less tolerant to alcohol, exacerbating the immediate and subsequent effects—for example, making us feel drunk more quickly, and giving us worse hangovers. It may even be more damaging to drink a great deal as we get older, since our brains change and age with us. At the same time, they start to become less resilient, and alcohol will increase the effect aging already has on our memory.

### *Do you honestly know how much alcohol you drink?*

## TIPS FOR SAFER DRINKING

- Don't drink every day.
- When you do drink, stick to the recommended guidelines for men and women. This does not mean drinking all your "units" in one or two nights. This is binging, and is not good for your mind or body.
- Invest in a bottle stopper so that you don't finish every bottle of wine that you open.
- Avoid drinking at lunchtime—your performance in the afternoon will be affected even after a small amount of alcohol.
- Avoid getting a hangover. Keep yourself hydrated by drinking water in between alcoholic drinks.
- If you do overindulge, don't drink for the next few days. Try to learn from it. Ask yourself Why did I binge? Was I anxious? Did it make me more uninhibited and have even less control over what was happening? Do I want that to happen again? If the answer to the last question is no, take some active steps to change your behavior.

## DRINK DIARY

It may be useful for you to figure out how much you actually do drink. Fill in the following diary for one week and then figure out the number of units you have had using the chart on page 125. You may find it useful to copy the chart below onto a plain sheet of paper and take it with you when you go out, so you can record your drinks.

|           | Lunch | Dinner | Other |
|-----------|-------|--------|-------|
| Monday    |       |        |       |
| Tuesday   |       |        |       |
| Wednesday |       |        |       |
| Thursday  |       |        |       |
| Friday    |       |        |       |
| Saturday  |       |        |       |
| Sunday    |       |        |       |

# HANDLING
# STRESS

*Stress makes us feel* tense and uncomfortable, even out of control. It comes in different forms—you may simply have too much to do, or there may be a specific event that has happened. It may be due to an ongoing cause such as difficulties in a relationship or living in noisy or crowded conditions. There are short-term causes of stress—being stuck in a traffic jam, for example—or longer-term causes such as a chronic back problem that makes sleeping difficult.

## HOW STRESS AFFECTS MEMORY

Stress is a major factor in memory difficulties, mainly because it keeps you from concentrating. In addition to preventing new memories from being formed, you may notice that your recall is poorer and you are less able to deal with anything complex.

## POSITIVE AND NEGATIVE STRESS

Stress is a natural reaction to life. We need to keep stimulated, and a small amount of stress (positive stress) can be useful. It can help us remain at the optimum level of mental arousal—for example, when we need to get an important report finished. When we have too much stress (negative stress), we become almost paralyzed and have a panic reaction. Then, unless we do something about it, life seems out of control.

| Positive stress | Negative stress | Short-term stress | Long-term stress |
|---|---|---|---|
| Causes: exam nerves, interview nerves, stage fright | Causes: too many worries or distraction, too much mental arousal | Causes: traffic jam, dental appointment | Causes: chronic pain or illness, unemployment |
| Effects: adrenalin flow aids performance | Effects: pain attacks, inability to function normally | Effects: minor physical and/or mental symptoms, which quickly subside afterward | Effects: constant physical and/or mental symptoms, which may become serious |

## PHYSICAL SIGNS

You may find that you also have a physical reaction to stress. You feel anxious and exhausted, you lose your appetite, you feel constantly distracted and can't concentrate, you become negative, your sleeping pattern becomes disrupted, and you often have intense dreams. Severe stress can lead to psychosomatic illnesses such as allergies, poor digestion, skin problems, aches and pains, mood swings, and so on. Although it is still not really understood clearly, chronic fatigue syndrome is considered by some researchers to be a condition exacerbated by severe stress—it is almost as if you cannot cope any more and your system shuts down.

### How to cope

To cope with stress, you need to develop a strategy. You must recognize the early warning signs and then learn how to manage the problem. First, you need to identify the cause.

- Is it your environment?
- Is it that you just have too much to do?
- Is there a specific cause at the present time?
- Is it exacerbated by your lifestyle?
- Are you managing your time properly?
- Are you able to "switch off"?
- Do you have a way of releasing the buildup of tension during the day?
- Do you have enough time for yourself?

Then try the following strategies:

- Make sure you are breathing properly (deep-breathing techniques can have a calming effect).
- Examine your life and make a plan (see page 69).
- Learn to say no (see page 72).
- Try relaxation exercises, such as yoga.
- Alter your lifestyle appropriately.

# PUTTING YOUR
## IMPROVEMENT PLAN
## INTO ACTION

*You are* probably wondering how you should proceed from here. When you have identified your memory strengths and weaknesses, and assessed all the other relevant factors, you will be ready to start improving your memory skills by implementing an action plan. To help you, the key points presented in Steps 1–9 are reviewed in the rest of Step 10.

# Getting started

## CREATE AN ACTION PLAN

By drawing up an action plan of your goals and strategies, you can start to figure out what you want to achieve and when. First, make lists of the following:

• Types of behavior that need to be changed or improved.
• All the situations and places where the changes are needed.

Now you should be able to finalize your plan. An example is shown below.

| Goals | Strategies | Timescale | Achieved |
|-------|-----------|-----------|----------|
| Remember names | Association, visualization | General | |
| Do better on exams | Listening properly, expanded rehearsal, meaningful learning | By June 1 | |
| Keep appointments | Use a planner, calendar, electronic organizer | Immediate | Yes! |

## START IMPLEMENTING YOUR NEW SYSTEMS AND STRATEGIES

To improve your memory using both internal and external strategies requires practice. You will need to:

- Measure improvements (a bit like assessing weight changes when on a diet). You have your test scores from Steps 3 and 4—go back and try those tests again now with your new knowledge to see if you have improved.
- Consistently use your new techniques—otherwise they will not last. Your improvements need to be tailored to you in order to fit into your lifestyle and be achievable.

# Keep going

## USE PROMPTS AND CUES

Write yourself notes to remind yourself to follow your system. Be organized. For example, don't leave your notebook behind when you go somewhere—you may need to write in it or to refer to it.

## BUILD REINFORCERS AND REWARDS INTO YOUR PROGRAM

At first it may be tricky, but just as by going to the gym you gradually improve your muscle tone, improving your memory takes time and effort. So make sure that you give yourself a pat on the back or a reward of some kind every time you feel you have achieved something, however small.

## GENERALIZE YOUR TRAINING

You will need to ensure that you "generalize" your training so that it gradually becomes more automatic. Try to use systems in various contexts. Spontaneous generalization tends to occur when you get used to new systems. For example, once you are in the habit of using a notebook, you will soon find that you can't live without one. That is why it is useful to number your notebooks in sequence from the beginning and keep them together, in order, for reference.

# QUICK
## REFERENCE GUIDE TO EACH STEP OF THE BOOK

*As a quick reminder,* here is a review of what you should have learned or achieved from reading this book.

### Step 1

You gained a basic understanding of memory. This is important because it provides a background from which to understand your own complex and ever-changing memory.

**Key points**

- The processes of memory take place in the brain. We encode information in different ways—through our eyes and ears, through touch and smell, and according to time, meaning, and importance.
- Short-term memory is for immediate information and is the gateway to long-term memory. It has an automatic filter system and has a limited capacity of about seven items.
- Long-term memory is our memory store, which is highly organized and needs to make sense of information to help us to store things better for easy retrieval. The more meaningful the information, the more effective the storage.
- We have different stores for remembering what we have to do in the future, for different time periods, for different forms of information such as facts or patterns, and for different episodes in our lives.
- We learn about the world explicitly, but over time, memories become automatic and implicit, which is why you can do things such as read, speak, find your way around, or ride a bicycle without any effort.
- Remembering is personal—the more personally meaningful something is, the easier it is to remember.
- We encode information in different ways—through our eyes and ears, and according to time, meaning, and importance.

## Step 2

You started to learn about what factors affect memory.

### Key points

- There are three main reasons why we forget: The memory fades and decays over time, new memories cause interference, and sometimes we cannot access memories from the store.
- We also sometimes need to forget, and this is quite normal.
- We need to be able to focus and concentrate to remember.
- Rehearsal is not enough to remember—you also need to form associations, give meaning to memories, and process deeply.
- We are better at recognizing than recalling, which is why, for example, we may remember someone's face but not their name.
- When we are trying to retrieve memories, sometimes we can't because of interference.
- Retrieval is aided by context and cues.
- Men and women are different and have different strengths and weaknesses.
- Sometimes there are emotional reasons why we cannot remember, such as repression due to an unpleasant incident, stress, or depression.
- Memory changes as we age. The optimum age for memory is sixteen to twenty-three.
- Increasing age changes our memory. Just as our bodies age, so do our brains, which causes memory difficulties.

## Step 3

You thought about your own memory and reviewed different facts that are important in understanding your memory in more detail.

### Key points

- No one has a perfect memory. We are all different, with varying strengths and weaknesses, so comparisons are not helpful.
- Other important factors should be taken into consideration, such as age, the importance of confidence, how stress and illness can be detrimental, and the fact that different personality types have different approaches.
- You completed an exercise to discover what type of optimizer you are.
- You considered your own personal motivation and goals.

## Step 4

You completed different assessment tests.

### Key points

- You tested your short-term memory: verbal, visual, and spatial recall.
- You tested your recognition memory.
- You tested your long-term memory: episodic and semantic.
- You tested your memory for the future (prospective memory).
- You concluded by filling in a chart to determine your own personal memory profile.

## Step 5

You learned more about the critical thinking skills you need to develop your memory.

### Key points

- Knowing your own memory.
- The power of concentration.
- The effectiveness of organization and planning ahead.
- Delegating, learning to prioritize, learning to say no, and leaving enough time for rest.
- The special ability we have to learn and the importance of integrating information to make it more meaningful.

## Step 6

You learned a number of different strategies to improve your inner memory.

### Key points

- Breaking down information into manageable chunks.
- Using organizational strategies.
- Organizing learning material.
- Making information meaningful.
- Using association strategies for learning, such as aide-mémoire and visualization.
- Using mental rehearsal to keep information in mind and get it into long-term memory.
- Using specific retrieval strategies, such as alphabet searching, category searching, visual searching, mental retracing, and context cuing.

## Step 7

You learned how to use external aids to improve your memory.

### Key points

- Planning your time and prioritizing tasks.
- Using organized systems and habits, such as a wall calendar in the home and office, a planner, a watch for timekeeping, writing notes to yourself, and making lists of things to do.
- Making realistic schedules and sticking to them (for example, when studying for exams).
- Learning to manage distractions.
- Becoming better organized.

## Step 8

This is a quick reference guide to coping with specific situations that commonly cause memory problems.

### Work situations

- Prioritize your day-to-day work. Make sure you make this a realistic plan so that you can actually achieve what you plan to do each day.
- Apply the eighty/twenty rule.
- Get organized—plan your week ahead.
- Manage distractions in your environment (forward phone calls, turn off e-mail, and so on).
- Arrange meetings or make phone calls in specific time slots.

### Everyday memory problems

- Remembering names: Listen, repeat, visualize, associate.
- Numbers and dates: Use and refer to a calendar, break numbers into chunks, try to visualize them.
- Losing everyday items: Form habits, mentally retrace, visualize, and get into the habit of always putting things in the same place.
- Forgetting what you went into a room for: In the first place, learn to concentrate and don't let your mind wander; otherwise stop and mentally retrace, or return to the room you came from to jog your memory.
- Tip-of-the-tongue phenomenon: Use alphabet search, use context and related cues and prompts, relax, visualize.

### Finding your way around

- Plan a route and visualize it before leaving, make a note of street names and landmarks en route, circle destination for easy reference.
- Ask directions—listen and don't worry what the person looks like! Summarize back to him, visualize, run through the instructions in your head, ask the person to slow down or repeat if he is going too fast or is not being clear.

### Studying for exams

- Listen carefully in all classes and lectures.
- Plan a manageable timetable well ahead of the exams and stick to it. Build in relaxation time and don't attempt to work all hours of the night.
- Divide topics into chunks, summarize, do extra reading to make them more meaningful, discuss with others, visualize, understand in your own mind.
- Give yourself rewards when you deserve them.
- Keep physically healthy—eat, sleep, relax.

### Managing memory lapses as you get older

- Stop worrying—this is the worst thing for your memory.
- Accept that as you get older, your memory will change a little and this is natural; discuss it with your friends.
- Check eyes and ears for conditions that may be exacerbating your memory problems.
- Keep mentally active with crosswords, games, discussion groups, reading, and so on.
- Develop internal and external strategies.
- If you are really worried about your memory loss, seek advice. This will either reassure you or ensure that you get medical treatment, if necessary.

**Step 9**

It was revealed how important specific lifestyle factors are and how much they can affect your memory. Remember, however, to be realistic, and don't be afraid of moderation.

### Exercise

Physical exercise is important because it releases positive chemicals in the brain that can stimulate memory function. Mental exercise is also beneficial.

### Diet

Moderation and balance is the key. A Mediterranean diet is a healthy one for mind and body. Include plenty of fruits and vegetables. Olive oil may help to protect from age-related memory decline.

- Foods that are high in saturated fat but low in nutrients are bad—80 percent of the nutrients in food are used by our brains.
- Specific brain-booster foods include proteins (such as fish, meat, dairy products, beans, and grains), carbohydrates to maintain glucose levels (fruits, vegetables, and grains), essential fatty acids (in oily fish), vitamins, and minerals such as manganese.
- Memory booster foods include red peppers, onions, broccoli, beets, tomatoes, beans, nuts, seeds, molasses, lean meat, and soy products.

### Alcohol

Alcohol has a powerful effect on memory and learning—it interferes with the brain's ability to form new memories. Remember that alcohol is a drug and safe limits should be adhered to. This varies from person to person and between men and women. Hangovers are caused by our bodies not being able to flush out toxins quickly enough, and because of dehydration, they make us feel dreadful, which affects our concentration and memory.

- Never binge drink.
- Have at least two alcohol-free days a week.
- Drink lots of water when drinking alcohol.

### Stress

High levels of stress are prevalent in society today and this can severely affect memory. Try to reduce your stress levels.

### Sleep

A good sleep pattern is essential for good mental and psychological well-being and functioning. Don't sleep too little or too much. Try to develop a sleeping routine that is right for you.

# RESOURCES

If you have concerns about your memory, contact a psychologist or neuropsychologist. These professionals specialize in the assessment and management of memory and cognitive problems, and can be found by contacting the **American Psychological Association** (www.apa.org). The following books are good sources of further information:

**The Handbook of Memory Disorders**
Alan D. Baddeley, Michael D. Kopelman, and Barbara A. Wilson (eds.)
An excellent academic and clinical overview of the area of memory by world-leading experts.

**Brain Food**
Lorraine Perretta
A guide to how different foods can enhance your brainpower.

# INDEX

# ACKNOWLEDGMENTS

**Huw Williams** would like to thank the staff and clients at the Oliver Zangwill Centre in Cambridgeshire for their helpful input on understanding memory and how to improve memory (www.mrc-cbu.cam.ac.uk/common/rehab/ely.shtml).

**Jo Iddon** would like to dedicate this book to her parents, and would like to thank Olly and Del for their unfailing support; her Cambridge mentors, to whom she is indebted for her knowledge; and her patients, from whom she has really learned the most. The Memory Assessment Centres in the U.K. can be contacted via their website (www.neurologica.co.uk).

Executive Editor: **Trevor Davies**
Editor: **Katy Denny**
Design Manager: **Tokiko Morishima**
Design: **Martin Topping**
Illustrator: **David Beswick**
Production Controller: **Jo Sim**